A Woman's Bike Book

Julie Harrell

An Owl Publication
NY 12040

First Edition

Printed in U.S.A.

Published by:
Owl Publications, LLC
New York 12040

Cover design and book layout:
Julie Harrell

Layout design assistance and quotes:
Mark Oppenneer (www.fineminddesign.com)

Photography:
Photo credits go to: Craig McMillan for the great cover shot, Tad Martin for the back cover shot and equally great time that day on the mountain and the river (go Tadmaster!), Jerome Tracy for the pic of me, Chrys and Reesa, Marilyn Price, Belle Marco, Inge Aiken, Jennifer Harvey, Jennifer Clunie, Kimberly Corwin, Sarah Seiler, Theresa Crombach, Jan Mares, Melissa Oliveira, Markham. All other photos, including bike shop and Kenda festival bikes, peeps and bling, were taken by the author.

Publisher's cataloging in publication data

Harrell, Julie A.
A Woman's Bike Book
1 Bicycles and bicycling—Women's sports

ISBN 0981877702 (Trade paperback original)

Acknowledgments

Once again, it's time to extend a gracious Mahalo to all my friends and associates who have provided their time, businesses, and photo efforts to ensure that this book would finally be published.

First and foremost, my family is just the best. Thank you all for loving me, for accepting me and sharing in this luscious life we live today on planet Earth. Reesa, my rides with you are the sweetest ever. Jerome, I love the way you throw yourself off the bike to avoid impending rock tattoos, and Alex, you make a fine mountain biker and you are even becoming a halfway decent bike mechanic. Thank you to my Ehmer family in Lawton, OK, and to Grandpa Reece in Arkansas. The many animals who are with us on our farm are also in my thoughts as I count our blessings. Thank you to my Native American and tipi meeting community. You have brought joy and Spirit into my life in a vibrant and wonderful way. Mother Earth, Father Sky, Brother Moon, Sister Sun. Water, Fire, Earth, Air. Mitakuye Oyasin.

My East Coast friends, including Chrys Ballerano who is just quite the mountain biking queen, you have made my life on the trails so much richer by your presence. Bob Priestley gave me a chance to work with him at Clifton Park Sports, and showed me the way down Plattekill Mountain. Paul at the Spoke showed me the sweet MA/VT trails and waited for me on the road. The shops I'd like to thank include The Spoke, Berkshire Outfitters, The Mountain Goat, the Down Tube and Mitch Plaine. Ya'll have always allowed me to romp freely through your shops, taking photos, fingering the merchandise and talking to your staff. I'll also offer here an honorable mention to the esteemed Tony Tom, at A Bicycle Odyssey. Without his patient guidance and kind spirit, I'd still be crossing derailleur cables just like that day in his shop when he first turned me loose with the tools. My riding buds in Marin County, California, Gail Weissman, Gravy, Barry, Dave, Joy, Penn and Arne, you took me down that yellow brick road and I never looked back.

I'd like to take a moment to thank all my bike shop customers who have inspired me to write this second women's bike book. By sharing my knowledge with you, I was able to enjoy your smiles once you got on the bike of your dreams for the first time. I listened to your questions and answered them all as much as I could in a non-bike jargon manner. I greatly appreciated your humor and sympathized with your frustrations. My customers, both women and men, I thank you for coming into our local bike shops. Lately I've also had the pleasure of hosting an Amazon.com blog whereby women from all over write in with their questions, and I attempt to answer them. I hope you keep writing, thank you for sharing both your joys and frustrations as you enter the world of cycling.

For those of you who are considering your first bike purchase, please remember this: Bike shops are still the only way to go. Buying a bike online may win you a few bucks up front, but your total satisfaction will be sadly lacking and you'll still need the shop to tweak your bike. Let's keep bike shops in business, shall we? It's the American thing to do! To all independent retailers, I am so glad you are still with us even though times are getting tougher and Big Boxes are getting bigger. May you always have fresh business coming through your doors.

Many of the photos in this book were submitted as a result of my plea for good pics. Thank you to all who have taken the time to send me such cool photos. If somehow I have left someone out, please contact me and I will include you in the next printing of this book. I'd also like to thank those of you who have so willingly posed for this book in photos taken by both me and your friends and family. Your energy and vibrancy shine through your smiles.

Disclaimer

The author does not accept any liability for decisions made by you, and recommends you meet with your local bike shop to assure proper fit and acquire other safety information. Find a local shop that works for you and be faithful to that shop. A helmet should be worn while cycling, but cannot eliminate all risks. Remember to check with your health care provider before beginning a new exercise, stretching and/or dietary program. This book is only for reference and entertainment. You are ultimately responsible for your own safety.

About the author

Julie, known as Jules, is mother to a wonderful daughter Reesa, and is happily married to Jerome Tracy, who has three sons. She has a M.S. in Technical Communication from Rensselaer Polytechnic Institute, writes proposals, and publishes regularly in the science, adventure, permaculture, and metaphysical fields. She has also worked in bike shops on and off for the past 17 years, beginning in 1992. After living and working in Marin County, California, Jules published her first book, *A Woman's Guide to Bikes and Biking*, in 1999.

Today, Jules is a member of the National Ski Patrol, and works for both Magic Mountain and Jiminy Peak. She also builds trails and rides backcountry with a local DEC ranger, and belongs to two local search and rescue teams. During the spring, summer and fall, Jules gardens, bikes, kayaks, skateboards and climbs until the snow falls. When trapped inside the house, she writes about outdoor adventures, permaculture and animal rescue, builds and rides longboards, tunes the family stable of snowboards and skis, and continues to build and repair the family bikes, as well as those of all her friends.

She is involved in local Native American groups, and lives a life of service to others. Jules is a yogic, chilled out mom, wife and farmer over 50 who is committed to living green and living clean. She welcomes your questions should you too decide to pursue this way of life. Please feel free to contact Jules at: photonicgirl@gmail.com

To order individual copies and get bulk discount books for bike shops and independent bookstores, please call: 518-265-2808 or write:

Owl Publications, LLC
PO Box 40
Cherry Plain, NY 12040

Foreword

By Marilyn Price

Welcome to the world of cycling and a journey that can transform your life. From simple fun and fitness to earth-friendly transportation, the time honored bicycle holds something for everyone. Whether on that dusty single speed in your garage or a new high-end rig, let the bicycle take you as far as you can go.

Why the praise for cycling? Biking changed my life and transported me to richer and more intentional way of living. I was raised in St. Louis at a time kids rode their bikes everywhere. I continued to ride my bike in college when it was less fashionable. I knew enough about the politics of oil that I kept on pedaling. Although I was a card-carrying environmentalist, I didn't really get it until I explored the Rocky Mountain on a mountain bike. It was on the trail at 10,000 feet that I truly appreciated the natural world I sought to preserve.

The bike took me further into the woods than I was able to tread on foot—in distance and at heart. One day while riding a trail up Mount Tamalpais in Marin County, CA, I had another Aha! moment—riding up mountains does that. As I scanned the expansive view of San Francisco, the Golden Gate Bridge, and Pacific Ocean, I thought about the inner city kids I knew in my social work. Wouldn't it be great if they could experience all this?

That was the beginning of Trips for Kids—a nonprofit organization that takes disadvantaged youth on daylong mountain bike adventures. What started in my living room is now a national organization with chapters coast to coast in the United States and Canada. The kids we take cycling are challenging themselves and are taking a closer look at nature. They are learning about life from the seat of a bicycle. And you can, too.

I was fortunate to find a way to turn my love for youth, the environment, and mountain biking into a program that is spreading across the country. When passions come together powerful things happen. I hope you tap into your inner adventure and make your dreams happen. Let cycling be a part of that journey. Maybe you will find yourself working your way up the race circuit or perhaps you will simply enjoy one ride that brings you great joy. Whatever the extent you experience cycling, this book will get you started.

Julie will introduce you to the many facets of cycling and take you to the streets and trailhead.

I have great respect for Julie and appreciate her cheering more women to the starting line. While living on the Left Coast, Julie was a Trips for Kids volunteer and ran our Green Cycling program. Her organized approach in this book will take you to great places with untold rewards along the way.

So take a ride. And like the kids who participate in our programs, fill your lungs deeply with fresh air and experience the newfound freedom and confidence that comes with riding a bike. You will become fit without even thinking of it as exercise. Moreover, you will be doing your part for global warming. There has never been a better time to grab your bike.

Once you are on your way, I invite you to become a part of the Trips for Kids movement. Volunteer in your local TFK chapter or if there isn't one nearby, consider starting one. You will soon discover the added rewards of doing things for other people.

Let this book be your guide to a new world. Enjoy the ride!

Marilyn Price
Founding Director
Trips for Kids

Contents

Introduction

"Get a bicycle. You will not regret it. If you live." Introduction to *Taming the Bicycle*

—Mark Twain

So you want to buy a bike. With so many styles to choose from it can be confusing at first, especially when you are differentiating between a comfort mountain bike and a race-ready hybrid, a road bike and a city bike, 26 inch wheels and 700c wheels (with almost identical tires). Let's not even talk about price! What makes this $300 bike different than the $500 bike? Should you buy women's specific models? Or should you just buy what the salesperson, your neighbor, your husband, your son, your uncle, your cousin tells you to buy? You might ask yourself who will ride the bike the most, and take it from there.

The good news is, the bicycle industry has rapidly changed in the past ten years, and the change is in your favor. Bike shops are now catering to the woman cyclist. More and women are buying bikes these days, and riding them wherever they please. You see them everywhere, riding down the streets, driving with bikes on their cars, hanging out with their girlfriends at the coffee shop, bikes parked nearby.

You could be one of them.

If you can sit on a bike, you can ride one. You can ride five miles or a hundred miles, it's really up to you. It doesn't matter if you aren't in perfect shape, because many women are carrying a few extra pounds. In fact, even if you are carrying more than a few extra pounds, your bike will help you get stronger, and might even decrease your appetite. We'll provide a few tips on what foods go down well when you are riding, and how to do a little yoga to stretch out those tired muscles. You'll feel confident as you walk into the bike shop, describe the type of bike you want to the saleswoman, and proceed to test ride and buy the bike of your dreams.

Sorting out those many bike styles is a piece of cake once you read this book, because it's all about what kind of riding you want to do, where and with whom. You might want to just take a little cruise down the flat bike trail behind the mall where all those other people are riding. You might have a gnarly mountain bike racer girl buried deep within your heart even though you are a grandmother. You could be a new mom who wants to pull her kids in a trailer and needs a bike that can handle dirt roads and potholes. Guess what! You are not alone. There are literally hundreds of thousands of women out there just like you, and once you get yourself the right bike, you might even decide to ride with some of them on the trail and on the road.

First, let's start with the basics of safety. We'll help you narrow down your bike choice, then help you get more comfortable within the bike shop. You'll find a bike that truly fits your body using our proven techniques, learn about proper cadence, which is efficient peddling, and finally, we'll teach you how to perform simple repairs to your bike on the road. At the end of the book are many resources to assist you in locating bike clubs and organizations where you'll meet nice people who also love to ride.

To make our experience more delightful, I have created a friendly group of composite characters to populate this book so that you can find your way into the lives of women cyclists like you and like me. Jules, even though she is a composite character too, is mostly me, as recognized by numerous goofy antics. The friendly women in this book are all sizes, shapes and colors, with varying degrees of physical fitness. Some are skinny vegetarians, others are husky women with robust appetites. To address the whole diet fitness thing, and to ensure that everyone starts on the same page, I've included two chapters that cover diet and yoga. These chapters are for those of you who may have a few extra pounds or a more than a few tight muscles. If you are interested in learning about what I've done in my personal life to overcome 40 pounds of excess non-muscle matter due to a former life of junk food addiction, these chapters are a great way to start where you are.

Now, whether it's raining or snowing or sleeting or otherwise acting up outside, I invite you to sit back and relax with your favorite cuppa, enjoy this book, laugh with us, cry with us, join us as we enter the twilight zone of women's cycling from a personal point of view. Yes, that's right, this book is personal.

1

The adventure

"Let me tell you what I think of bicycling. I think it has done more to emancipate women than anything else in the world. It gives women a feeling of freedom and self-reliance. I stand and rejoice every time I see a woman ride by on a wheel...the picture of free, untrammeled womanhood."

—Susan B. Anthony, Women's Suffragist

Let's ride, shall we?

You see an IM message on your screen from Sally. It says "Hey, want to go for a mountain bike ride?"

"I can't," you IM back, "I'm working."

"I'm working too," Sally IM's back. "Just checking your reflexes."

"That's not funny," you respond." You know I hate being tempted while I'm trying to make deadlines."

"I gotcha that time," Sally IM's back. "What I meant was, let's go for a ride tomorrow evening after work. I'll gather the girls together and get back to you."

"Okay, great plan. TTYL," you respond. But the seed has been sown, and now you are absolutely dying to get on your bicycle. Which bike should I ride today? you ask yourself, staring at the array of bikes in your house. Can't stand to have less than three in the kitchen where you work as a writer, the stepchildren having taken over your former office. The bikes serve as a not-so-subtle reminder that you are free to ride like the wind at the drop of a hat.

The old school Voodoo Wanga mountain bike stands waiting for you. That thing looks absolutely gnarly with its fat new Marzocchi fork, knobby tires and bar ends. You ride a serious hard tail mountain bike because that's what it takes to handle the trails where you and the girls like to go. Fat BMX pedals allow you to ride without special shoes, and besides, while bushwacking on the trail when it becomes rocky, it's much easier to tromp through the mud with hiking boots. Your thoughts become olfactory as you suddenly smell the trail with its thistles, the weeds now bruised and broken by your steps, the dust and dirt and flowers and trees. The trail beckons, calling you.

Hold on, reality check. How smart is it to ride alone on a trail out in the middle of nowhere? You of all people should know better. Remember when Mary fell and bruised her arm so bad she couldn't hold her handlebar and everyone had to walk out with her? What about the time you popped a wheelie over a log then flipped backwards and hit your head? Took you a few minutes to realize you'd cracked your helmet, good thing the girls were with you that day. Mary had her ibu and it helped a lot. Okay, maybe a mountain bike ride around town is a better idea than a mountain bike ride out in the woods alone. The smell of the forest recedes and new thoughts crowd your head as you gaze at your road bike.

Hmmm, it's a beautiful day outside, sunny, 70s, not too much wind, could be a great day for a road ride. The sounds of traffic reach your ears as you ponder. Riding with cars is just not fun, besides, I need to put new tires on my road bikes before hitting the pavement again, you think to yourself. The mountain bike still beckons. You feel like your bikes are calling you from both sides, making it hard to decide. Meanwhile, the clock is ticking and the day is passing you by. The work you started has piled up even higher on your desk as intense bike ride daydreaming briefly takes hold and lures you away from your desk.

You pick up the sweet new Specialized Armadillo road tires and finger them. They were expensive but will last for several years. There's nothing like the thrill of heading downhill at 50mph and knowing your tires won't blow out. Gosh, it's so tempting to saddle up and ride out the door this minute. Wow, that was a close call. You head back to your laptop and continue working. Those bikes can wait, you tell yourself. You silly machines be quiet for a minute and leave me alone so I can work. Later that morning the clock strikes 12:30, lunchtime. You finish your paragraph and realize that three hours have gone by. You get up, stretch your back, and decide that it's time for a bike ride for real. They have been vibing you anyway, beseeching you to take them out for a spin, even a short one. But you know better than that, when it comes to rides, you have to have several hours to truly get your fix.

Okay, here we go again, now which bike should I ride, you wonder. I'm leaning towards the road bike, but wearing road shoes is just not that much fun. The gravel driveway isn't conducive to skinny tires either. It might be challenging to walk around stores if you decide to visit favorites, the Mountain Goat for gear and Wild Oats for some organic snacks. Patagonia is having a sale, maybe Amy at the Goat will have something nice to wear on sale. The thought of shopping is the motivation to get on your road bike. Finally! A decision is made.

A lightbulb flashes in your mind, how about riding with Keene sandals? Or taking the Teva flip flops in the Camelbak? Either or will allow you to walk around and still ride with style. Okay, a plan is made, you will do a tri state ride from NY to VT to MA and back. Glad that decision is made, twenty five miles, two hours and shopping in between. That sounds great, as none of your girlfriends are available midday for a ride anyway, but you still desire the company of people. Time to change those tires.

The Mountain Goat

You get out your Pedros tire irons and pop those puppies off. Tssssstttt! You have the passing thought that it's great to know how to change tires, true wheels and adjust headsets. Life would be so challenging without basic repair skills. Take old tire off wheel, place tube inside new tire, place one side of new tire on wheel using tire irons, pop the other side into place. Inflate slightly, check tire for bulges, inflate to full pressure.

In no time at all, the tires are replaced, pumped up to 120 psi, back on the bike and ready to roll. Floor pumps rock, don't leave home without one! You let your tires and wheels sit for a moment because you never know, even the best mechanics get pinch flats now and then. Looking at the tires closely, you spin the wheels of your bike one more time. Nope, not a bulge anywhere, we are good to go. Grabbing a few Powerbars, filling up the Camelbak and gathering together your road tools, you head for the car. The Topeak Alien is indispensable as an emergency road tool, and if you discovered you didn't have it, you'd most likely head home and get it before taking to the road. The helmet, some bike shorts, an extra tube, a spoke wrench, some cash, the credit card. These are all packed into your Camelbak and into the under the seat bike bag.

No surprise, your Toyota truck is full of kayaking gear. Take the kayaks out of the truck and place them upside down on the grass.

Get out the Thule truck rack, place it on the truck, give it few twists, then take the front wheel off your bike. Clamp the skewer down on the front fork, and jump into your truck. Time to roll!

Ten minutes later you are bouncing down your very rocky driveway. Your plan is to drive part way so you can quickly return to the truck and pick up your daughter from school. Ten miles north towards Vermont, you park in a gravel parking lot, and get your stuff ready. Excitement and adrenaline build as you ready your gear for the solo journey that will involve a lovely smooth flat road that follows the river, with hardly any cars, an uphill climb past farms and fields and cliffs, then a fast descent into Williamstown. This is the perfect solo ride and it's a beautiful day outside. You get everything ready and at the last second put on your biking shorts. They feel like a diaper and you've never enjoyed wearing them except on the bike, where they are required gear. Otherwise, ouch! After a few quick stretches, you jump on your road bike and hit the road. Pedaling along at 70 to 90 rpms, a fairly fast pedaling pace you discovered long ago in Oklahoma, you breathe deeply of the summer's scent.

Wildflowers bloom along the river, you can smell the spray. Hmm, wonder if the wave is up, you think to yourself. You stop a few miles down the road and hike down the riverbank to check out kayaking possibilities. Nope, not up today. The clear, blue green river is low right now, not much rain. You recall when you were there only two weeks ago and it was raging over the banks, with hidden strainers and dangerous whirlpools. What a difference! It was too high to paddle, now it's too low. Pausing for another moment to admire the wonderful scene before you of a quiet still river, you enjoy the silence, the purple and yellow flowers, the bumble bees and the soft sounds of the water rushing over rocks.

Solitude has its virtues.

Climbing back into the saddle of your road bike, you head up the rolling hills of Vermont. Getting into the grove, you pedal faster and faster, increasing your rpms to about 85 versus pushing harder gears. Even though you are pedaling fast, your legs are less tired than if you were pushing harder gears and pedaling slower.

Here's why: Now that spinning classes are popular, more and more women understand the dynamics of pedaling and its effect on our physical body. "It's always good to spin," you think to yourself, saving your knees for rock climbing and of course, snowboarding. There will be more on winters in upstate New York later. Speaking of pain, your forty-something neck kind of hurts. You keep thinking of changing out that old Salsa stem on your Masi road bike and replacing it with a stem that has more rise. Sure would decrease the neck pain, but also would decrease your ability to do what you are about to do, which is go really fast downhill.

You get onto the highway which has a huge shoulder, click into high gear and tuck down. Your body remembers how to tuck from years of road riding, and does so automatically as you increase speed down the long, straight hill. Ahh, that's what that low handlebar stem is all about, the tucked position. You continue to increase your speed, rolling faster and faster until you are at 50 mph just zooming, flying like a silent bird down the highway into town. Oh man this is the biggest thrill of all on a road bike, tires barely touching the pavement, heart beating wildly, you maneuver your bike around road debris while remaining in the tucked position, and continuing to push higher gears. The world no longer exists outside of you, those precious two quarter inch spots of tire rubber on pavement, and your trusty steel steed. You know that at this speed, a blown tire, loose handlebar, loose wheel, broken chain, loose headset would spell disaster, which is why you always go over every last piece on your bike before taking to the road. The wind whizzes by, cars and trucks pass but you take no notice. You are a bird in flight on a wide shoulder, cruising at 54mph. Life is glorious! And the tires hold.

Once you approach town, ten minutes later, you take the first side road as this road just got busy and the shoulder shrank to less than a foot. It's time for you to detour onto the quiet back roads strewn with stately houses, big wide yards and old oak trees. Silently, you spin along. Your bike is so quiet you can't hear a thing. Most women don't realize how easy it is to maintain their bicycles. If they did, you think to yourself, they'd all do it. Reaching the downtown area, you cruise to the Mountain Goat and park your bike on their deck. The owner comes out to greet you, and you both step inside, chatting about winter sports adventures. Amy's a cool lady who built a play kitchen for her three kids so they can hang with mom at the Goat. Snow's a coming, you assure each other.

You check out one of the Trek women's mountain bikes, seriously considering it for your daughter. It's not a ladies model, per se, but a re engineered bike with a woman's body in mind. That's one tough looking bike, but it has a sold sticker on it. You stroll around, fingering the Kavu clothing and Patagonia slacks. The Marmot lightweight jacket catches your eye, hmm, that's a sweet little package, would be great for backpacking. A half hour later, you take your purchases to the counter and pay for them, leaving them stashed at the store till you return with your car. Amy kindly refills your Camelbak with water, and you decide to forgo the health food store and instead pedal on down to The Spoke, your favorite East Coast bike shop.

The Spoke

The vibe at The Spoke is decidedly different than the Mountain Goat. Loud heavy metal music fills the air, while the staff of two college kids rib each other wildly. You park your bike inside, slip into the bathroom and wash your face. When you come out, some guy is already fingering your road bike.

"That's quite a styling ride," the cyclist says admiringly. After all, the Masi 3V is a classic Italian road bike. What makes your bike so interesting is that the stickers are in Russian. The guy with the fingers is on a Felt road bike, complete with Dura Ace everything. You admire his bike, too—in fact, you have a Felt road bike and your husband has a Felt mountain bike, both purchased at The Spoke. Paul took a chance with a small company that only sells high end bikes. That was a smart business move, as those things are sweet. "What's that puppy weigh?" you ask.

"Like, 18 pounds," he says. You both gaze at your pet bikes, enjoying the view. Meanwhile, laughter from the shop reaches your ears. You wander over to the mechanic station to see what's so funny. Paul was telling one of the guys about the time Big Al made some chick wipe out and you know it's you being teased.

"Hey Jule," he laughs. "Remember that first ride with us when you got all muddy and almost bailed out on us?" Your brown eyes meet his blue eyes, old friends from way back.

"Uh, dude, if I recall that was you who wiped out behind Big Al and then you whined like a baby for the rest of the ride." The gang roars, you got Paul good that time. In reality, it was you who fell into the mud, but hey, a quick retort is required if you want to hang out in a bike shop.

"All right, dude," he says, smiling, "you owe me some beers for that one." Beer is the currency of choice amongst the young adventure crowd. Paul comes out from the mechanic station, wipes his hands and give you a hug. It's been a while, old friend. You huddle around your bike, talking about the virtues of a more upright stem, but he convinces you in no uncertain terms to leave the stem you have on your bike. After all, the Masi was meant to go fast and that doesn't necessarily mean it's super comfortable.

Finally, you leave the shop, tired but happy. Now you have to ride home, zig-zagging through short cuts to reach your highway again. Man that was fun, you think as you climb up the highway shoulder. The traffic has slowed and you have more room on the road. Soon, you approach your turn and are back in Vermont, pedaling past cows, flowers and the blue green river. Another day gone, and it was a good day because you rode your bike.

By the way, want to know what really happened with Big Al? Long ago and far away, a young lady moved to upstate New York from Marin County, California. She said Dude a lot. Check out Chapter Eight, "Riding with the guys," for the full story.

2

Yoga for all sports

"Life is like riding a bicycle—in order to keep your balance, you must keep moving."

—Albert Einstein

Getting started

I admit it. Shiva Rea inspired me to dance. She's my favorite of all the home yoga teachers out there that I've experienced. Why? My feelings after spending time with Shiva's DVDs is that she brings me to a place of spirituality in my yoga practice. Yoga has become as important to me as any of my adventure sports. I used to have a bad monkey on my back if I couldn't do something really scary almost every single day. Now, I'm mellow because I always have a plan.

It's a typical winter day, cool, cloudy, wet, drizzly New England mountains. Cold. Very windy. Time to feed the llamas and goats and run back indoors. Gosh I had planned to go for a hike with the dogs but it's just yucky and besides, I have yoga tonight. I'll get some exercise. It's so tempting to go outside.

Do I want to go outside or shall I remain inside and practice yoga? After all these years of having to having to just HAVING TO go outside I now have something I can do inside and feel good about. After all these years of being a wild adventure child, I can be content with a purple yoga mat placed in a small space in the living room, with the fire going in the fireplace, and my limbs stretching to places they've never been before. Let me tell you a story:

I was at a great ski resort a few winters ago, being my silly slippery self, and waiting to hop on board a quad lift (one of the big ones) to go way up the icy mountain side so I could silly slide on down again. Ah what fun to breathe the Adirondack fresh air, what fun to chat with my guy acquaintances during free tele lessons as I learned the proper way to make finer turns. I just wanted to go play but I tried hard to pay attention to what they were saying as we got on the lift together all of a sudden, unexpectedly an icy ooops!

I fell on my butt, well no worries, I'll get up in a second, it's kind of hard with loose heel skis still attached to my big plastic boots. What's that, wait a minute, the lift is still moving, it's rolling over me O My Goddess it's rolling over me my hips are now vertically aligned, I'm being rolled by this huge monstrosity, a woman screams, she sees me under the lift, it keeps rolling me I'm not that hipless, it comes close to totally crushing my pelvis breaking my back but wait a moment. I roll, effortlessly into a spinal twist as the lift churns slowly around and leaves me horizontal again.

I breathe a sigh of relief as the lift finally stops, someone noticed and turned it off just outside the nick of time because my time was up two minutes ago. While it squeezed me and moved my hips my back my body I flowed with the machine. All the backbends and twists I've done with Shiva in front of my TV have served me well this day, as there is no crippling injury, no ambulance, no sirens. No surgeries. I've moved my body rather than broken it. I'm in my forties, not that limber but limber enough to be absolutely bendable.

In fact, I'm fine. I jump up, free from the thousands of pounds of moving steel that has twisted my body totally around in front of a live audience. I jump on the seat. Are we ready to go guys? Hey, what's the big deal, I say in general. Those tele skiers, someone in our now good sized audience murmurs. We are now airborne and off we go.

I'm just not coordinated, but at least I'm flexible. Recently, I fell in front of the post office on some ice, twisting and contorting my back into a weird pretzel shape (I don't fall well). I was completely unhurt. I attribute that to regular yoga. This winter is my second attempt to learn snowboarding as I just learned how to link my turns last spring. It's obvious after two full days of falling on the icy snow here in barely snowing New England that I still have a long way to go to get it. Other than sore muscles, I'm not hurt at all and as I said before, I don't fall well for someone who does so many sports.

Ladies, yoga will save you. Just do it. In Shiva's words, "Start where you are." First, a disclaimer. Don't feel like you have to hurt yourself to be doing yoga the "right" way. Scan your body, assess your energy, and modify your poses to honor injuries. For example, I'm currently dealing with shoulder problem from whitewater paddling this past summer, so I have to be careful with arm balances. I have noticed that these somewhat modified arm balances actually are helping my shoulders recover, but that's because I'm being thoughtful to ensure that pain means stop. Please discuss any new exercise routine, including yoga, with your health provider to ensure that it is right for you.

The good news is, I'm a beginning yogi, so my stretching routine is within the reach of most reasonably fit women. I know women who are less fit than I am and much heavier, and they can stretch even further so it's not necessarily about your size. Depending on what you can handle, the following routine is a great way to warm up and wind down before and after a long day on the bike. Here's a basic routine I practice. Who knows, it may save your life someday.

If you can't immediately join a yoga class, which is optimal, I recommend purchasing the DVD entitled *Yoga Shakti*, by Shiva Rea, for her rendition of Salutation to the Sun. The Salutation to the Sun, "Surya Namaskar," includes many stretches that are easy to execute and will sooth your muscles, preparing you for that burn that comes with gentle, moderate and hard exercise. The Solar Sequences are refreshing and will awaken your spine to the new day. The Lunar Sequences are calming and relaxing, and more conducive to a good night's sleep after a long day spent adventuring.

Salutation to the Sun

First, remember to breathe. Breathe through your nose and start where you are. Don't force any of the poses, because you don't have to. Yoga isn't about pain, it's about gain. Eventually you will open up and become more limber.

Begin with Mountain pose, Tadasana

Mountain

Stand erect with both hands at your sides, feet parallel, calmly facing forward on your mat. Keep your back long and straight. Breathe. Inhale, and raise both arms over your head, stretching them up to the sky. Breathe, feeling the blood rush down through your body as you hold this pose.

Exhale into Standing Forward Bend, Uttanasana

Forward Bend

Bend forward, with your back straight. Keep your hip joints directly above your ankles and let your arms fall towards the ground. Your hams will burn and you may not be able to touch at first, which is okay. Don't worry, you will stretch with gravity, just let it flow. Ah, breathe. The goal is to reach the floor and place both hands firmly in front of you, so you can hold your body steady for the next movement. Exhale, and lunge backwards with your right foot. Hold that pose. Bring your left foot back and place it next to your right foot, both feet parallel, holding your weight with your shoulders and toes. Inhale, bring your left foot back, matching your right foot, back straight, not arched, and breathe.

Inhale, exhale, then move into Cobra pose, Bhujangasana.

Cobra

First on your belly, face down. Breathe for a moment, exhale, then lift up with your arms, leaning your head back as you stretch into an arch. [A gentle variation of this pose is to keep both forearms on the floor. I use this variation most of the time as my shoulders are sore from whitewater paddling.] While in this position, your body should lie supine onto the floor, elbow over hands, face down. Feel the stretch in your back as you arch, drawing your shoulder blades into your back and lifting your chest.

Inhale, again, exhale, back to the ground, your body supine onto the floor, elbow over hands, face down. Inhale, come up on your arms into a stretch, lean your head back, elbows slightly bent. Feel the stretch deep in your abdominal muscles. Your shoulders are feeling the weight of your body.

Exhale into Downward Facing Dog, Adho Mukha Svanasana.

Down Dog

In this pose, you have both hands and both feet on the floor. Your back is arched, stretched up to the sky, while your legs are straight, with knees firm but not locked. Your feet are both facing forward, heels touching the ground if you have the flexibility. Both hands have fingers facing forward, with your middle fingers pointing directly in front of you. Hold the pose, and breathe.

Inhale, lunge forward, landing with your right foot between your hands, left foot extended behind you. Keep your knee over your foot.

Exhale, Standing Forward Bend, Uttanasana.

Forward Bend

In this posture, your head is hanging down and you relax your muscles, just let them go. Hold the pose and breathe. You should have a little more flexibility in your back, so allow yourself to bend forward more if that is comfortable for you.

Inhale, Mountain, with arms overhead. Tadasana.

Your feet are together, eyes facing forward as you reach for the sky with your arms. Feel the stretch.

Exhale, Mountain, with hands in Namaste.

Repeat the sequence, only this time, lunge forward with your left leg. Perform these poses several times, working up to ten rounds per day. Eventually, you will discover a lightness of being that you never thought possible. If you can, find a yoga class near you that you enjoy, and spend time with other people feeling your body grow stronger. Enjoy the newfound freedom that the practice of yoga brings to your life. Namaste.

3

My favorite diet

"Burn Carbohydrates, Not Hydrocarbons"

—Bumper Sticker

This chapter introduces the concept of what foods go down best before rides to avoid nausea and lengthen stamina, and what foods are optimal to ingest after rides to fill the belly and recover. We'll even include a couple of yummy recipes of my own.

The following eating information is strictly for informational purposes only, and reflects my own personal experiences as a hungry cyclist. These days, I really don't even eat cheese anymore, preferring instead an almost vegan diet which includes a little buffalo or venison about once per month. I also am not much into eating bread, preferring whole grains instead. Back in the old days though, I needed to move from an almost entirely junk food based diet more into a really healthy, burnable diet. By not giving up all of the foods I loved, I was able to gradually modify my cravings to where they are today. Hence, the bagels, chips, cookies and cheese you will see below. If you ride, you can eat. Plain and simple, you can eat some stuff that you might think is disallowed in a traditional weight loss "diet."

My personal experience is not intended as health advice and should only be followed if you personally enjoy eating the way I do. I am not a doctor and wouldn't claim to be a nutritionist, refusing to follow anyone's idea of "proper diet." I eat carbs and olive oil and think they are great. In fact, I lost 40 pounds following my own wacky but healthy compared to the old days diet of 2000 calories per day.

With moderate exercise, anything less than 2000 calories a day will probably cause most people of my size (135 pounds, 5.8) and activity level to lose weight. I do not believe and will never recommend eating 1200 calories per day, so if you are looking for a skinny girl quick fix you are in the wrong book. Food's a great thing. Let's eat it.

Bonking and puking

Worthy of mention is bonking and puking. As a cyclist, I have bonked on many occasions and learned to always carry food of some type, even if it's only in the form of a few old raisons stuck in the seat bag of my bike. Never, ever go without food on a ride. Once you have bonked, you'll find it incredibly difficult to finish your ride. I have bonked on several memorable occasions during long rides back in Oklahoma.

On one ride in particular, my girlfriend and I had plotted out a 95 mile ride, not taking any food, and skipping our first 10 mile pancake stop. We instead planned to visit a store in an unknown small prairie town 30 miles distant. Guess we were trying to lose weight or something. Well, there was no store in the town we plotted to ride through, so instead we luckily bummed some soft drinks from the people who used to run the store. Oklahoman's are a friendly bunch of people, especially out in the boonies. Anyway, it was at the 75 mile mark that we finally found food that day. There's a famous little restaurant in Meers, Oklahoma that serves the best pecan pie in the world, along with huge quart sized drinks. We careened into the store, ordered two pieces of pecan pie apiece and proceeded to sugar up on pie and soft drinks. Then we had to climb the hill out of there and pedal another 25 miles home. To say we felt poorly is an understatement. My stomach still cringes at the thought of that entire day, fueled only by sugar, cramped and pained at every pedal stroke.

Another time I set out with the Big Boys on a hard road ride through the Wichita Wildlife Refuge. None of my best friends were in attendance so I was at their mercy and they could care less whether I stayed with them or not. I stupidly forgot to bring a snack of any kind and was totally I mean totally bonked about 30 miles into our ride. I reached a point where I couldn't pedal anymore at all. The guys took one look at me and just left, never to be seen again that day. I was alone, walking along a country road when I happened to see a house. In that part of Oklahoma the houses, especially inhabited ones, can be far apart. What to do? Well, after hitchhiking around the United States as a young woman, I was unafraid of approaching strangers for a snack, especially since I was completely unable to pedal my bike and knew I didn't have the energy to walk all the way back to Lawton, where I lived at the time. So I crept up to the door and softly knocked. A friendly farmer face answered, looking at me quizzically. I said, "Sorry to bother you sir, I've ridden my bike this far, and I ran out of food. Now I can't ride home!

Guess I looked pretty pitiful to him but he didn't really know what to make of me so he just looked at me. "Can I please have a few slices of bread?" I asked. Now I'm sure you think I'm a real loser but the fact is, bonking is bonking and sometimes you have to beg for food! He went inside and brought me two slices of bread and if memory serves, a banana. I gratefully thanked him, scarfed the food and rode my bike home, newfound muscles in my legs and arms. The moral of these stories? Never go without food and never ever ride with people who won't offer you a Power Bar if you bonk.

What really goes down well

The following foods that are described are all organic. It's possible, if you look hard enough, to find health food stores, or buying clubs, in your area. You may have to drive 100 miles but then you can stock up on dry and grocery items and eat healthy at home. We keep a large amount of rice and grains available at all times. We buy locally from farmer's markets and coops to ensure that much of what we eat is fresh and healthy, and also to support our local economy.

Unless you live and bike somewhere like Oklahoma, hot cereals are great for pre-ride breakfasts. If it's hot and you are riding in the heat of the summer, a bagel with natural peanut butter provides long term energy. If it's cold outside, or you live in the great Northeast, there are several ways to make hot cereal and have a solid breakfast. Some of my favorite recipes are made with one of the following organic dry ingredients: polenta, steel cut oats, ground brown rice, multi-grain cereal, some of which can be mixed with the following: granola, raisons, maple syrup, cayenne pepper (yes a little is great for you) and cinnamon. You can always add butter but many of us are watching our butter intake so only add a little for flavor.

Some of us have also been known to eat the breakfast of champions, pasta or spaghetti, add black pepper, olive oil and fresh basil, skip the tomato sauce. This is the type of breakfast that goes down well and keeps your body moving for a long time. Another great is white or brown rice with some Parmesan cheese and a little salsa or hot sauce. MMMMM! And coffee is an awesome boost as long as you limit your intake, otherwise it's to the bathroom we go, every fifteen minutes or less.

What doesn't work well for most women before a long hard ride are the traditional breakfasts of pancakes, sausage, cheese, eggs, bacon and toast. Somehow the eggs get churned up as you ride and climb and uh, you get this sort of bleh feeling in your gut. Your muscles don't seem to work as well as they should, your legs feel heavy. Eggs, bacon and toast are fine for *after* your ride, but we'll get to that in a moment. Another pre-ride no no is a big bowl of ice cream. Hey, women have been known to indulge from time to time. What happens is that sugary, creamy, dairy extravagance becomes a leathery, broiling, boiling dead weight that is churning and burning your gut as you ride. Plan to barf as you peddle uphill because there's no getting around it, that stuff will come out, regardless of the strength and resolve of your intestines.

Another crazy food mistake is fat, buttery cinnamon rolls and sugary jelly doughnuts. They hit you like a ton of bricks then take forever to digest. By the time you finally get the stuff moving usefully through your bloodstream rather than blocking your arteries, the ride is almost over, the sugar low has struck and you haven't enjoyed a single pedal stroke. Even the loyal PB and J, if overdone will cause you major grief. Think you are so hungry you can eat two? You'll soon regret that decision. The bike is one area that just doesn't leave you room to overeat.

Now, with all that said, the good news is, if you really like sugar, you can eat all kinds of previously off limits foods once you've ridden twenty miles or so, especially if you are continuing to ride another couple of hours. Chocolate chip cookies and M&Ms start to look mighty tasty even to those who eschew sugary snacks. Stopping at a pre-arranged spot to have a nice cup of coffee and yes, perhaps a cookie is a great way to reward yourself during a long ride. Some people even consume sports drinks although they've never worked for me, I need a lot of water. The bad news is that sugar is really not healthy in any form, so you are better off not eating candy bars on the road or otherwise.

Recommended bike ride foods are not sugary snacks, as it's much healthier for women to eat their carbs in fruit or grain form while riding. For example, taking a few bananas in your pocket will get you over the low potassium hump. Peanut butter sandwiches are a longtime favorite, as are any one of the multiple granola bars and sports bars on the market. I generally throw cash, several Cliff Bars and some licorice into my Camelbak. Depending on how far my friends are riding that day, we'll all take something to share with each other and have a feast.

A lesson learned in Marin County California, back in the 10 hour plus mountain bike ride days is, never refuse food on a ride. Even if it's just a bite or two of the proffered melted chocolate bar in someone's grimy mud splattered hands, take it. You may discover that on down the road, when you've run out of food, that piece of melted muck pulled you through. Plus, another thing, it's always good to pack a little extra for those who forgot to pack their own. Because I guarantee you, these skinny stragglers will appear on longer rides. They are the starving bonkers on a pseudo diet that doesn't work, begging for nibblies.

Plan your meals

Generally speaking, I like to eat a lot of calories before a ride, something carb with maybe dairy (like rice with veggies or mac and cheese) after a ride, then veggies and soup in the evening, or low fat protein such as grilled salmon with potatoes. In other words, eat a lot in the morning, moderately after your ride, then taper down in the evening and eat lightly. What happens after a ride is you may come home totally starved so it's best to pre-plan. If your husband cooks like mine does, ask him to prepare something that will coincide with the end of your ride so you can scarf and munch healthily instead of grabbing the fresh loaf from the breadmaker and stuffing yourself with that and a stick of butter. Yes, that's happened to me and it could happen to you, too.

First and foremost, keep a food diary. In your food diary, also record what you did that day for exercise, even if it is only about cleaning out the cat box. Well, maybe you don't need to mention that, but if you took even a brief walk, write it in your diary. I personally use a Tidelog, published in Bolinas, California every year. It shows the tides, the moon, the meteors, and has room to scribble what I ate along with appointments. Having this food diary allows me to see how my weight fluctuates over the long run, and also to keep track of how much exercise I'm getting. Back in the day, I wrote neatly and carefully. Over the years these little notebooks are getting a little sloppier as I've been keeping a food diary since 1984. My weight has fluctuated by 5-10 pounds, but that's reasonable considering it's been 18 years since I permanently changed eating habits. Some people might find the following diet a little weird, others may have an "Aha!" moment as they recognize that this is the diet of the active woman. To prepare you, first I'll tell my own fat girl story.

I was fat since age 16, about 40 pounds overweight. I knew that my body would follow my spirit, but I wasn't sure how to get thin again. So every day, in my affirmations, being a spiritual person, I thanked God for my healthy, thin body, even while filling my mouth with literally half gallons of ice cream. The mind knew what the body forgot—my subconscious knew it could pull me out of the fatness abyss. Daily affirmation is key to success and we'll talk more about goal setting and affirmations later in the book.

Food is medicine

According to some, food is medicine. Yet, we are bombarded with greasy fast food and heart attacks in the United States. Weird combination, when you think about it. To be healthy one must consume what the body needs, not what the tongue desires. A simple test will determine what is good to eat: If you consume a cheeseburger, McFries, and a McShake, do you immediately go do your favorite exercise like biking? That is not recommended, at least by me. The difference between a pre-workout and a post-workout meal should be only in the quantity of food consumed, not the quality. Basically you need to eat healthy 99% of the time, be it breakfast, lunch or dinner. A simple test answer is, to lose weight and be healthy, if you can comfortably exercise on a certain type of food, you can eat it. Good food = happy, slender, healthy body.

It's not easy to eat right, especially in the beginning. I used to work in fast food restaurants and I ate everything in sight. Once I gave up that line of business, I was left with the detritus of fast living, an extra 40 inglorious pounds. To help myself learn how to eat better, I created a specialized diet, just for me. I now weigh 135. The best way to follow this diet, should you decide to give it a try, is to include exercise, such as walking and biking, at least four times per week. Gardening counts too. Start out walking around your block twice per week if that's all you can handle.

Groceries

Take a trip to the local healthy food store and buy some groceries. Items to buy are: ten pounds of rice, hominy grits, oatmeal, creamy rice cereal, split peas, lentils, pasta, pasta sauce, pesto sauce, natural peanut butter, honey, bagels, salsa, apples, bananas, dried fruit, salad mixings, white potatoes, sweet potatoes, carrots, cabbage, onions, garlic, fresh ginger, spices, popcorn, herbal teas, olive oil, balsamic vinegar, unsalted peanuts in the shell, healthy corn chips, and yes, Fig Newtons. Ditch the diet sodas and buy sparkling mineral water. This list can be varied, but you get the picture. Plan to pre-cook your rice, prep your soups and salads, and take your lunch to work. And, most importantly of all, begin a food journal to keep track of what you eat. If you follow this plan, modified to fit your lifestyle and favorite foods, you will feel more energetic, get sick less often, and enjoy a healthier body.

Note: Try to purchase locally. Here in New York, we have a lot of homegrown crops, such as squash, corn, apples, pumpkins, to name a few. Find a farm stand or farmers market, and buy food that is grown where you live. At all times, try to buy organic, because now, on top of pesticides, we are eating genetically engineered foods that are designed to not replicate themselves. Think about it, if the food can't reproduce, how well will your cells reproduce? I question any and all attempts to bioengineer crops to suit the larger chemical corporations financial interests. Who's going to look out for your body? Only you.

Recipes to quell the blues

Veggie toast with peppers

- sour dough bread
- cheese, sliced thinly
- tomatoes, garlic, onions
- jalapeno peppers
- red bell peppers
- fresh basil

Take the garlic, smash it and finely chop it. Chop the basil, onions and jalapenos. Slice the tomatoes, dice the red bell peppers, and slice the bread. Toast one side of the bread, remove and spread a thin layer of tomatoes, onions, red bell peppers, jalapeno peppers and basil on it, then broil again on the untoasted side. Remove, spread cheese and garlic on top, then broil again until cheese is melted, and slightly browned.

Mark's lentil soup

- 2 cups lentils, soaked overnight
- onions, garlic, jalapenos, mushrooms
- carrots, green bell peppers, potatoes
- tamari sauce, oil, butter,
- fresh rosemary, paprika

Bring lentils to a boil, and simmer for at least two hours. Finely chop garlic, and jalapenos, then pile them together and put them aside. Chop onions. Grate potatoes with skins, slice carrots, and mushrooms; dice green bell peppers. Saute potatoes in oil with onions, add soy sauce. Saute carrots and green bell peppers in oil with rosemary. Lightly saute mushrooms, garlic and jalapenos in butter. Once the lentils have simmered for two hours, add all the sauteed veggies, and simmer for one more hour. Serve with toast.

Julie's split pea soup

- 3 cups of split peas, soaked overnight
- carrots, purple onions, garlic, celery, zucchini squash
- fresh basil, fresh cilantro, fresh rosemary
- tamari sauce, olive oil, sorghum molasses
- cayenne pepper

Bring split peas to a boil, then simmer for three hours, adding water occasionally and stirring. Slice carrots, celery, zucchini squash; chop onions, garlic, basil, cilantro, and rosemary. Saute carrots, celery, zucchini and onions in oil, then add tamari sauce and cayenne. Lightly saute garlic, basil and cilantro in olive oil, then add rosemary. Add all the sauteed veggies to the split peas, and simmer for one hour. If you like cheese, grate a little Parmesan on top of your soup.

Julie's peanut butter-granola muffins

- 1 1/2 cup peanut butter (the real stuff)
- 3/4 cup maple syrup
- 1 cup soy or rice milk
- 1 cup flour
- 1/2 cup oats
- 1/2 cup granola
- 2 tablespoons baking powder
- 3 eggs

- 1/4 cup oil
- Chinese cookie seasoning

Preheat oven at 350 degrees. Mix all dry ingredients thoroughly, and keep them separate. Mix all wet ingredients thoroughly, then quickly fold everything together into dough. Place 1/8 cup amounts of muffin dough two inches apart on greased cookie sheet, then bake for 12 minutes, or until brown. These yummies digest fast and keep well on hiking, biking, climbing or surfing expeditions. Enjoy!

Julie's fresh pesto

- 2 bunches fresh basil from your garden
- 1 cup olive oil
- 1/2 cup Parmesan cheese (optional)
- 1/2 cup pecans, cashews, or pine nuts
- lots of chopped garlic
- cayenne
- tamari sauce

Chop basil and garlic, add nuts, Parmesan cheese, tamari sauce, olive oil, and cayenne. Put everything in a blender and blend until a thick green paste is created. Use this absolutely luscious pesto sparingly on noodles if you are watching your weight, or pile it on with gusto and forget the calories. Speaking of piling it on, I prefer to eat pasta with my pesto :)

The non-diet diet

This is a my personal seven-day plan that is very useful if you have a cold, the flu, or just want to clean out your system. Everything in the non-fruit, non-veggie, non-rice category has to be consumed early in the day, preferably two hours before exercise (optimum time is three o'clock in the afternoon). You must force yourself to eat heavily once per day, to the extent that you are truly satisfied beyond piggery (stuff yourself). The nice thing about this particular eating plan is that you will lose weight within the first three days if you are overweight. You can eat a meal of your choice with meat and some (not much) dairy, and some (not much) greasy fried junk once per week, to feel as though you haven't given up the beauty of your previously unhealthy lifestyle. Those arteries can't get clogged with only a once per week attack of junk food.

Chocolate is allowed, as is a bit of candy and a bite of cookie, but remember, that doesn't mean the whole Toblerone or the entire bag of Oreos. You should limit excessive fats of the solid kind, attempting to eat only four hundred fat calories per day, max, unless you are eating on peanut days (more on peanuts later). The thing to remember is that since you are used to high fat, highly 'satisfying' foods on a regular basis, sort of like 'reverse reward' foods (they reward your hips with cellulite), that particular craving must be dealt with early in the morning, first thing. Fat satisfies. The right fat satisfies enough to energize you for hours and hours; the wrong fat makes you barf at the top of the hill when you try to exercise after a McMeal. If you have any allergies to peanuts, etc, please substitute almonds or other nuts/protein that you can eat. If you are like me, and no longer eat dairy, just remember, sugar is the next culprit that could be eradicated from your diet. Anyway, enough of the lecture, here's my personal seven day plan that left me 40 pounds lighter. Most people can live with something this yummy and easy for at least a week. What have you got to lose except a few pounds?

Days One, Two and Three

Breakfast	One cup of uncooked rice (cook it) with a handful of peanuts in the shell and a bagel.
Snack	Three or four cookies, a Power Bar, chocolate, etc.
Lunch	One cup of uncooked rice (cook it) with some raw veggies, tamari sauce or miso.
Snack	Cookies or corn chips.
Activity	Enjoy your favorite sport or take a walk.
Dinner	Veggie soup, big salad, huge amounts of fruit, no fats or real carbs.
Snack	A bite of peanut butter with hot tea and honey before bed.

Days Three and Four

Breakfast:	One cup uncooked (cook it) hot cereal such as oats, grits, creamy rice or wheat with raisins, honey, or jam, and a bagel. Or: Two bagels with four tablespoons of peanut butter, toasted in the oven with raisins. A handful of peanuts in the shell. Mmmm....
Snack	Air-popped pop corn, chips, cookies, chocolate, Powerbar. If you eat the bagel-peanut butter-peanuts breakfast you won't be hungry.
Lunch	Huge salad with fruit, veggie stew. Or: Milk or yogurt and an apple if you have the peanut breakfast (okay, have a little dairy)
Snack	Cookies, candy, chocolate, chips.
Activity	Enjoy your favorite sport or take a walk.
Dinner:	Pasta with low-fat sauce and a salad with maybe a dinner roll.
Snack	Have an apple.

Days Five and Six

Breakfast	One cup uncooked (cook it) hot cereal such as oats, grits, creamy rice or wheat with raisins, honey, or jam, and a bagel. Or: Two bagels with four tablespoons of peanut butter, toasted in the oven with raisins. A handful of peanuts in the shell. Mmmm....
Snack	What are you eating for lunch?
Lunch	Huge salad with fruit, veggie stew. Or: Milk or yogurt and an apple if you have the peanut breakfast (okay, have a little dairy)

Days Five and Six (Continued)

Snack	Air-popped pop corn, chips, cookies, chocolate, Powerbar. If you eat the bagel-peanut butter-peanuts breakfast you won't be hungry.
Activity	Enjoy your favorite sport or take a walk.
Dinner	Pasta with low-fat sauce and a salad with maybe a dinner roll.
Snack	Have an apple.

Day Seven

Breakfast	Hot cereal.
Snack	What are you eating for lunch?
Lunch	Anything you want, just pig out on the low-fat items and tread lightly on the greasy kid stuff. Yes you can have meat. Only a little cheese, please. Absolutely no ice cream.
Snack	Are you really hungry, or just munching?
Activity	Enjoy your favorite sport or take a walk.
Dinner	A huge veggie plate or salad.
Snack	Fruit and hot tea, of course.

If you eat this way for at least seven days, your body will have a chance to rejuvenate and heal itself. Fresh herbs cooked with vegetables like the ones listed above will do wondrous things for your body. Now for my rant, and ladies, please bear with me. When you eat in this manner, you no longer need to rely on Tums and Ex-lax to 'regulate' your body—it will regulate itself. To the Asian communities around the world, food is indeed medicine. In fact, recent research demonstrates that food (such as overuse of sugar) can cause cancer and food (healthy organic vegetables) can fight cancer. Many Americans find it hard to drastically change their diets and visit their local Asian doctors—this is understandable, because old habits die hard.

It's sometimes difficult to resist the lure of Whopper Deluxes, double chili cheese fries, and chocolate shakes. Since most Americans suffer the effects of improper diet and no exercise, pesticide and pollution often gang up with these factors and wreak havoc on our bodies. Then, we take too many antibiotics, over-the-counter-of-dubious-value medicines, and a host of prescribed anti-depressants, stimulants, laxatives and diuretics, hoping to recover our health. Combined with overuse of medications, x-rays and multiple yet unmatching medical diagnosis, not to mention the monstrous BILLS for all this activity, we are a nation headed for health crises unlike anything since the Black Plague.

Can we save ourselves? Certainly. If we embrace a healthy diet that includes the occasional sweet treat or slice of cheese, seek out practitioners of Asian and natural medicine (there are many American M.D.'s who practice and/or support both), take responsibility for our own health and realize that food is indeed medicine, we can return to the Garden of Eden and enjoy true, ever-lasting health. As Hippocrates once said, "Let food be thy medicine and thy medicine food."

Last but not least, enjoy yourself! A nice cold beer or two goes down well after a long hot day on the bike. A glass of wine takes the edge off after a cold hard mountain bike ride in the woods. You can be like me and have a non-alcoholic beer and still enjoy yourself. Whatever tickles your fancy, eat, drink and be well.

4

Your bike

"Don't buy upgrades, ride up grades."

—*Anonymous*

Choosing your bike

Bike manufacturers have created new names and categories to describe what is in my mind, bikes that still fall into about three main categories. If I thought I could even begin to do justice describing all the bikes of the various top companies such as Trek, Specialized, Diamondback, Jamis, Giant, Serotta, Terry, to name only a few—I would attempt to use everyone's categorization systems. Instead, rather than attempt to gather all the names together of all the manufacturers, I'll provide my own classification system of the different types of bikes available on the market today. I have not included every single type of bike one can purchase, nor do I detail bikes such as old style single speeds, three wheelers, recumbents, tandems and unicycles. These are available though, so if you are seeking a special type of bike, don't hesitate to ask your local bike shop for assistance in finding the right bike for you.

There are essentially three styles described in this chapter that a woman can choose from, then subcategories within each of these styles. Each bike design subcategory is based on price, rider position, and intended use.

Comfort bikes

Miriam has a jones to just chill on her favorite flat, paved bike trail. True, she's packing a few extra pounds but she's very fit and also happy with her body shape. Who says big isn't beautiful? Not her man, he loves her and in fact, is afraid that if she rides too much she'll lose that gorgeous goddess look that he so craves. So Miriam's all set, she just likes to ride her bike on the paved bike path with her friends. They do occasionally have the urge to go fast over the speed bumps. Mary and her friends mainly like to ride a few miles, stop and smell the flowers, sit on the bench, talk about life, ride a few miles more, stop and have something to eat. Miriam packs a mean lunch of dried tomatoes in olive oil, fresh mozzarella cheese, fresh Italian bread from the local bakery and yes, a half liter sized bottle of good red wine that she picks up at her favorite store in town. It's a fairly rare local wine, and absolutely wonderful. She has special plastic wine glasses.

Miriam's girlfriends usually accompany her. They all have the same bike, a Specialized woman's model that cost between $400 and $500, depending on which model each woman chose as her favorite. The bikes have fat bald tires, a woman's frame with a sloping down tube, a big woman's saddle for their wonderfully large derrieres, and upright handlebars with cushy grips that also have a shifter attached. The bikes are purple, green and yellow, and the girls are Miriam, Pam and Sharon. All good friends, all happy cyclists, all women of size who are proud of it and love to have their weekly ride with a tasty lunch in the middle of it. Doesn't that sound like fun? Hope they invite me someday. We'll call their bikes *women's comfort bikes.*

Comfort hybrid

Same bike as Miriam's with skinny 700c tires. Women or men's models are available and have a similar geometry although the women's models tend to be even more upright than the men's models. The seated position is ramrod straight. Comfort hybrid bikes sport skinny wheels and tires that are larger in diameter than the 26inch wheel comfort mountain bikes. These bikes go a bit faster but trade off speed for handling, meaning they do not handle bumps and ruts well. The upright rider position combined with skinny tires is optimal for riders who want to remain on the bike path or on flat streets, rather than attempt to climb long hills or ride many miles. This super comfy bike is great for around town, slightly faster than the fat tire version, and a little more squirrelly due to the skinny tires and larger wheels. This bike has many names, but I call it a comfort hybrid bike, genetically engineered for the suburban mom with a little time here and there to cruise the neighborhood with the kids. Great for exercise, the $400-$500 *comfort hybrid bike* is available at most local bike shops near you.

Road bikes

Aggressive road with dropped handlebars

Jules has got to gnarl. She's probably barking up the wrong tree but she loves to go fast and has this racer baby background so even though her 50 plus year old neck would prefer a more upright position, she's still riding these hardcore aggressive take the money and run bikes. She's on an Italian steel road bike that positively screams on the downhill but hit a bump oh baby there's absolutely no mercy cos you are gonna go flying into the ozone and then when you finally hit the ground oh pray hard it never happens, you will be a goner. And your bike will be toast. Totally. At her age she should be looking at a different riding style instead of screaming downhill at 53 mph. As a friendly customer once said, Neck pain isn't yogic. He's so right.

Jules is riding something fast and lean and mean and painful that's twitchy and touchy and tweaky and the slightest little nothing she's off the road into the brush. There is no mercy here. She just loves it and goes home to treat her sore neck with a long hot shower, Chinese plasters and arnica rub at night. On weekends, she visits her favorite spa and sits in the whirlpool with the jet right against her neck. Sure there are road bikes out there that are a bit less hardcore, and she could always get a more upright stem and have a nicer ride but a slower day. For now, since Jules won't budge and insists on sticking to the old school style ride, we'll call that creature an *aggressive road bike.*

Aggressive road with flat handlebars

Betty likes to ride her bike to work. She's got a lot of stress because she's a corporate attorney in a big firm and works downtown. Traffic is horrendous and there's no parking at all. Sometimes she has to work late at night on briefs and then she's dealing with the danger of street life in parking garages after dark. She's already been stalked a few times, called the police yada yada and pretty much had enough of dealing with walking to her car after dark. Betty's a single thirty something woman living in a big city with a high paced corporate job, no real life to speak of other than her career (she may make partner in her firm if she can work long enough hours) and she really needs to have something in her life other than work. One day, after yet another close parking garage incident, Betty decided to take matters into her own hands and bike to work. There are advantages when biking to work. Her company has showers and she's got her own office where she parks her bike, so she can hammer to work and still arrive freshly showered for her multiple morning meetings that stress her out to no end but at least she got some exercise. On that fateful day during the hour long lunch she allows herself, Betty strolled into her local downtown totally boutique bike shop and picked out the perfect $1500 bike for her very fast ride to work and home. Betty needed something lean and mean that would go very fast and take some abuse.

She's now stylin' big time on a Specialized road bike with flat handlebars and a body fat index of under 10%. This bad girl bike is solid black, with nothing extra on it but a couple of bar ends for climbing hills. It has skinny 700x 23c tires, weighs in at under 22 pounds and goes fast. The flat handlebars allow Betty to see what's in front of her and handle the bumps that only a big city can dish out. Betty is in an aggressive forward lean position that puts her in control and leaves little to the imagination. She's riding clipless pedals with a small Camelbak pack, an C02 inflator in case of a flat, a tight jersey, shorts, tights, shoes and nothing else.

Betty prefers to travel light and have her bike serviced at the shop where she bought it rather than worry about maintenance. She takes her little machine in once a month for a tune up because she abuses it so badly on the city streets. She's got special liners in the tires to ensure that she doesn't have to deal with a flat late at night after delivering yet another brief to another high profile client. Betty can ride her bike through town faster than she could ever drive, so her car remains parked in the garage while she gets fitter and fitter riding fast in and fast out.

Oh, and by the way, she saw her harasser walking down the street one day, same guy who stalked her in the parking lot at night. She rode up to him feeling pretty mad, and she was looking tight with all black with a black helmet, gloves and shoes. She got right up next to him silently, before he even realized who she was.Betty said, "You ever even so much as look at me again and you are going to eat my bike pump." The yucky would be harasser literally ran down the street to get away from her. Funny how city life can be sometimes. One minute you are getting stalked, the next minute you are confronting your stalker. Betty now has much less stress in her life and by the way, she just made partner in her firm. She is an aggressive lady who rides an *aggressive road bike with flat handlebars.*

Cyclocross

This is the perfect bike for everything. You can bang it you can toss it you can carry it around. It's got a fat/skinny frame with dropped handlebars, the frame is so tight it puts you right over these handlebars with your arms down low on the handles. The cyclocross bike is available now with disc or cantilever brakes, 700cc knobby tires, two to three front chain rings and plenty of attitude. This bike goes fast and can handle a variety of rough stuff, including city pavement, dirt, trails and creeks.

Whether or not you want to ride this level of variety on a bike that looks like a road bike with fatter tires, I don't know. Should you take the cyclocross bike where it's intended to go, out on the race trail that is also used for mountain bikes, you'll discover what it's really like to ride the trails without any extras. Cyclocross is old school European racing at its finest.

This type of bike has been around since before mountain bikes were invented, and can be compared to mountain biking as soccer might be compared to football. A cyclocross bike can be used by the experienced rider for fast down and dirty city commuting, and for bicycle messengering. They are around $800 up, and well worth the price. A *cyclocross bike* looks somewhat like a fat road bike, or a squished up touring bike. The sharp angled seat tube and frame geometry demands an aggressive riding style and will get you where you are going very fast. I wish I had one of these babies. Maybe then I'd quit riding my Masi road bike off road.

Touring

Diana always dreamed of graduating from college then riding across the country before settling down into a "real" job. People kind of thought she was crazy to do this on her own, but Diana believed that seeing the world from the vantage point of a bike saddle would allow her to experience the beauty of the United States in a personal way. Besides, riding a bike was better than spending ridiculous money on gas and gaining a bunch of weight from eating car food.

While finishing her degree, she saved quarters in a big gallon pickle jar. Each quarter was one step closer to fulfilling her dream of riding across the United States, from the East Coast where she was at school, to the West Coast, where she intended to live. When the jar was full, she was ready to buy her bike at the local bike shop.

Diana had been staring at that bike for a long time, because it just sat there gathering dust. No one wanted a touring bike these days, she thought to herself, but look how beautiful it is. The bike was long and sleek and wide and stable. It was forest green with fat 700c wheels, broad dropped handlebars, an upright stem, brazons for panniers, a triple crank with a low low granny gear. This sturdy bike would handle mountains with steep uphills and downhills, and carry her and her gear for thousands of miles.

The guys at the shop knew how much Diana wanted the touring bike so they sort of saved it for her, not encouraging customers to look at it, letting it gather dust in the hidden corner in the back of the shop. This bike was for Diana, and she finally came in one day and bought it. She bought a Bob one-wheeled trailer to haul her stuff, along with a set of panniers for the back of her bike. She also bought a case of peanut butter Cliff bars, extra tubes, tires, an Alien tool and a black spoke wrench just in case she popped a spoke. The guys at the shop gave Diana a sweet deal on all her gear as she was a poor college student and a loyal fan of their shop. They wished her bon voyage and took photos of her before she left.

Diana sold most of her possessions, packed up her gear, got on her bike and set out for her dream ride across the country. It's been a long summer, but last I heard, she was wrenching at a bike shop in California, writing a book about her trip and surfing during the week. Diana rode all the way from Amherst, Massachusetts to San Diego, California on a *touring bike.*

Mountain bikes

Recreational hard tail

"How about a short loop?" Patricia wrote in an email to her friend Sally. It's been a half hour and there's still no reply. I'd love to have some company, she thinks to herself, simultaneously reviewing her favorite online recipes for pot roast dinner. Everyone would be home from work and school by 4pm, so getting dinner together was a top priority.

Hmmm, mashed potatoes is a given, add peas or salad? Sarah hated peas and Bob wasn't about to touch iceberg lettuce. But iceberg and peas was all she had in the house. Then there was the bike ride to consider. How could she pull together dinner and avoid an afternoon trip to the store, Pat wondered, getting the roast out of the freezer and setting it on the cabinet to thaw.

If I don't get out of the house soon I'll never make it out for me, and get in a bike ride, she muses, puttering around the kitchen. Cookies, a few cookies will make me get out and ride, she decides, grabbing her favorite expresso chocolate chips out of the cabinet. MMMM! Lightbulb! Okay, choices. I can ride my mountain bike to the store and get the stuff everyone likes, thereby avoiding family squabbles for a change. After all, that's why I bought the bike!

Fast forward: Pat's riding her stylin' city bike, well, what she considers a city bike which is actually a recreational mountain bike with semi bald tires and panniers...to the grocery store. There's nothing special about this bike that stands out to the casual observer. Ah, but behold closely, and you will see what makes this bike Pat's favorite around town ride. This recreational mountain bike can be bought for under $400. Giant is an excellent company that caters to this particular market, providing a great bike with a low top tube.

The low top tube means you can be 5.8 with short legs or 5.6 with long legs and still ride the same bike. It fits short guys with long legs, short women with long legs, tall guys with short legs, tall women with short legs, etc. [See Chapter 6, the bike fit section, for more details on why geometry makes this bike special.]

Pat bought her bike off the shelf at her local bike shop after describing exactly what she intended to do with it, which was go to the grocery store several times per week (hey, gas got expensive) and ride it around town doing errands. She click shifts, jumps curbs, hits potholes and dodges taxis, no problem with this simple but tough little mountain bike. Pat named her bike Mojo, cos she's got her mojo on when she rides it. We'll call this one a *recreational hard tail mountain bike.*

Aggressive hard tail

Oh baby, forget about work, this is so much fun! Miles from nowhere, out in the wooded New England mountains further than the eye can see, Jessica laughs as she boofs another rock, whitewater paddling style. Her tires are mushy, her shock has six inches of travel and she can jump five feet into the air off a rock on a downhill without crashing going very fast. This is just like telemark skiing in the trees, whitewater paddling on class III creeks, snowboarding off the ice bowl what a rush!

Jules is below, already having boofed the rock, bunny hopped the log at the bottom and turned swiftly left uphill, quickly shifting down into granny in the back, stayed in second on the front, onto the leafy single track, oops! She's off her bike, did an endo over the handlebars off the hidden log, she's big time into the mud.

"What happened, are you okay?" everyone asks, anxiously rushing to their fallen comrade. Yes, fully conscious, she's fine, her helmet took the hit, knee is scraped, shin bruised, wrist sprained, personality slightly stunned, muddy butt. "Dang. I slammed into that tree," Jules muses, still a bit confused about what happened. "Ouch!"

Mary hauls out her girl's first aid kit, vitamin I for cramps, and hands Jules a couple. Sally grabs her iodine tablets for when they have to drink skank water if they are desperate, and Betty gets out her climbing gym tape. Sally holds up her Camelbak with the tube facing down and squeezes the mouthpiece to pour water onto Jules' scraped and freely bleeding knee, then grinds an iodine tablet into the wound cos there was some cow patty where she wiped out, actually she wiped out in the cow patty (yeaoooch!!!).

"There there, you'll be fine." Betty then expertly tapes up Jules wrist and soothes her with promises of a sweet ride up yonder, pointing to the big pine forest where it smooths out into alpine tundra up top where the lightening strikes.

In case you are wondering, after she made partner, Betty got another bike and joined this group of crazy women. She met Mary at the local coffee shop, started talking about gear and bikes, then, supped up on a triple expresso latte with soy she sprinted across the street and bought herself a sweet ride with a fat shock and all XT derailleurs. It cost $1800 plus some for a ultra light Felt aluminum hard tail from her local boutique shop. She rides it to work in the wintertime and on the trails with her girls in the other time. Oh baby it's some sick stuff and they totally rock. This is called *aggressive hard tail mountain biking.*

Aggressive single speed

What will you do with this in hill country with only one gear? I have no idea but it sure looks like fun. Trialsin? Jumping logs? Riding BMX trails? Just like when I was a kid. Is this really a 26-inch wheel BMX bike in disguise? I'll ride one if someone gives me one. Just call me. Better yet, send me an email. I'll come pick it up. I'll bring a six pack for ya. This is an *aggressive single speed mountain bike* and yes, please, I'll take one. Immediately.

Aggressive full suspension: Downhill

Betty. She's so bad and she's really too old to get away with this at thirty something but what the heck, why not live a little anyway.All that angst and stress in corporate attorney land and nowhere to spend it but on a bike. She bought her third bike, a $3k full suspension downhill mountain bike and started doing lift serve at the local ski resorts with some guys she met at the bike shop. Take the lift up, ride your bike down. Cheap summer thrills.

Betty had a little stress to relieve and some serious skills developed during her years riding her road bike in the city and her mountain bike with the girlfriends. She found out that down hilling allowed her to really deal with what was bugging her as it required so much concentration that she couldn't even begin to think about work while she was doing it. The guys liked having her along as she pretty much never wiped out and could hammer them down any slope at any speed.

Short story long, Betty got into bike racing and is now a state champ going for the nationals. She's working hard at her new job, which is riding her mountain bike full time in Colorado. One day, Betty started thinking she'd rather ride hard than anything in the world. She was sitting at the office, all dressed up in her corporate look, daydreaming about riding instead of working. While musing about riding, Betty realized she was always in the front of the pack, road or mountain, male or female and damn that felt good.

Betty was one strong athlete and had had enough of those stinking corporate meetings with endless litigation and angry clients and awful partners with fat guts, strong martinis and big steaks and they kept trying to get her to go out with them but they were boring. The idea started to take shape in her mind that there was something more to life than money and wearing a suit downtown. She worked late and went home to a lonely apartment filled with bikes. They welcomed her. She touched the mud on their wheels and the knobs on their tires. They spoke to her about a better life that could be lived if only she had faith. Betty came to work early the next morning to yet another mean email from the boss, decided she'd really had enough, and jumped on her bike to ride home.

There she was in the middle of the woods, fully suited up, ready for a day out on the trail alone, which was unusual for her but it had to happen. By now she carried a full assortment of gear and tools and could repair most mishaps that might happen with her bike and everyone else's, so she was unafraid of the elements and competent as a mechanic. Betty started thinking that the trees and the woods and the hills were more important than that ugly high rise building with smelly carpets, dank air and bad water. She decided then and there, about ten miles into her mountain bike ride, to quit her corporate attorney job to race mountain bikes full time. Who'd a thought it would ever happen to her? Or that she would drop everything just cos she got on a bike one day extra expressed on lattes? It happened.

Betty's now a full time racer babe, and she's sponsored by Jamis. They gave her a bike and pay for her race entry fees. She wears full on protective gear just like you see on a motocross rider, complete with full face helmet, padded shoulders, chest, elbows, thighs and shins. She's living in a studio in Colorado with some women who also mountain bike and all she does is spend her time training for the next race and drinking beer with the locals. Betty's loving life to the fullest because she's beyond hardcore. She trains in the mountains out west and is ready to race all over the world.

Betty doesn't ride anything ordinary although she still keeps her city bike and hard tail mountain bike around for recreating when there's time. She now rides a $5000 full suspension downhill mountain bike with eight inches of travel, front and rear. She rides over stuff most people wouldn't even walk over. Betty's so crazy that she won't even blink at a ten foot cliff as she totally snags the rock and slinks down the cliff somehow not wiping out then screams around the trees back off another cliff up over a log down a stream under a rock over a bump. And she's good.

This is her first winter here out west, and the snow's awesome. Betty's starting to eye whitewater kayaks as her next venue, as they say the creeks really run hard in Colorado in the springtime. She's already bought a harness and shoes because the climbing in Eldo is sweet they say and there's a new man in her life who wants to take her there. Betty's riding a *full suspension downhill mountain bike.* It's heavy, it's tough and it's made for serious experience.

Cross country

Poor Jules. She really needs something with some more give. She just doesn't have the balance to put it all together. Wreck after wreck, and still no mercy from the mountain. Some people can ride down 45 degree angle creek beds with running water and moss covered rocks but not Jules. She train wrecks on the stuff, every time. Or lately, she just walks it. What to do?

Well, Specialized has a sweet Epic ride out that just totally rocks. It's super lightweight with all the travel front and back that a girl could ever need. You can lock it down for going uphill then let the shock loose for downhill. Jules is thinking this may be the next ride for her, but the cost is sort of prohibitive, around $3500 for what she really wants. And she's already got five yes, they are all fairly old school and beat, but still good bikes in the basement that she rides.

Who can justify a sixth bike, and a fourth mountain bike? What to do, what to do. Should she buy the bike, be a total consumer, give in to the gear lust and finally stop crashing? The pro is, with this new bike, she can finally ride with the big boys. The con is, she's an old schooler who barely tolerates having a front shock with all the requisite maintenance, much less a rear shock. Who's got the tools for this stuff anyway? not Jules. You gotta send it back to the maker to be fixed, like yearly. What a hassle!

But that creek bed really hurt on the last crash. She dented her thigh and banged her elbow. The boys rode on, not knowing she wrecked yet again. Or knowing, who knows. Jules is seriously thinking about getting another bike, and it's that beautiful Epic sitting in her favorite shop that's just her size. It's ready for her to ride it uphill and downhill and all around hill and maybe, just maybe, the mountain will have more mercy on her if she's riding a new *full suspension cross country mountain bike.*

5

The bike shop

"When I see an adult on a bicycle, I do not despair for the future of the human race."

—H. G. Wells

A good bike shop shouldn't be hard to find. In keeping with a great phrase, "Think globally, shop locally," begin your search from your house and visit the closest bike shop. You may have a nice one right down the street. Branch out, ask around and check out the shops a bit farther from home. Your favorite shop might be a bit of a drive but worth it. Find a shop and stick with them. Now for the good news: Women are beginning to populate shops more and more, and shops are catering to the girl crowd because they realize that we, ladies, are the women with a mission. Here's the other news: You still need to be prepared to deal with the general attitude that can prevail at some shops that are actually exceptional otherwise. That is, testosterone territory.

Okay, so you walk in and you can't stand heavy metal music. The guys are sporting nose rings, you can see pizza crusts and yes, and empty bottle of some microbrew, and the clothing rack has (eek!) dust on it. A good shop might seem like macho guy world where only roadies with shaved legs and neon jerseys hang around, swapping crash stories and admiring their scars and a woman can never enter. Wrong. Just walk on in like you own the place. I'll tell you how to do it.

A good bike shop may be that little hole in the wall that doesn't sell tricycles, has European racing frames hanging in the window, and a bathroom that smells like, well, someplace to be avoided. A good bike shop can also appear as a sparkling, well-lit place with beautifully polished wood floors, artfully marketed displays, clean bathrooms, and a staff with matching black polo shirts. You aren't looking for appearances here, although they certainly help the uninitiated. What you are looking for is great service, people who know what they are talking about, and who are willing to share information with you. You are also looking for a one year service warranty on a new bike, which includes the basic tune-ups for one year after purchase.

Remember, the people who greet you at the door may also be the shop mechanics. If they seem surly they probably haven't been able to get out on their bikes enough this season, so bear with them. Good service is what you are looking for and they are the holders of the good service keys. Increasingly, bike shops are also employing women who ride, are gnarly, or ride, are mellow, or ride, are of the chunky variety, or ride not, and are still great sales people. Just give the shop a chance, and go with their flow. They may have a groove you could learn from and they may have a bike you will love. You are not shopping at Wally's here folks, as your local bike shop is a privately owned enterprise, homegrown in America. Let's support them, shop locally, and ride free.

The typical bike shop with a management that rides with the employees, supports its local race team, and employs people who dress in an alternative manner, may not fit into the conservative model one expects to find these days in contemporary shopping. A brightly lit, finely tuned shop with all the sparkles of a large, corporate department store may seem more inviting to the first-time bicycle buyer. You don't have to look far to find a good shop. You just have to look carefully.

Great shops treat their customers with respect, take the time to answer questions, and enjoy repeat business from loyal customers. They also employ people who love to ride, which does cut into shop hours, making them slightly less accessible to people who can only shop on Sundays. Truly great shops may look like grimy bike messenger hideaways on the outside, but if you look carefully, you will discover a wealth of information right beneath your eyes. So go ahead and stroll into the shop that strikes your fancy, whether it is a clean, well-lit place, or a roadie hangout. You are now about to become armed with the conversational tools you require to negotiate your way into the bike of your dreams.

First impressions, as I said earlier, can be deceiving. The very woman-friendly owner may be out buying cappuccinos and donuts for the surly but genius mechanic who greets you at the door, or doesn't greet you at all, which is sometimes the case. Go ahead and stick around, check out the bikes, and see what they seem to be selling. Is it mainly mountain bikes, or mainly road bikes? Do you see any obviously used favorite bikes that don't seem to be having repairs but are parked around like little pet cats? Those probably belong to the staff. Are they mountain bikes or road bikes?

Your initial inspection will tell you more about the shop if you toss any preconceived notions of how the shop should appear. You are more interested in whether they really know much about bikes, whether they all ride or not, and what they ride. If you are in the market for a road bike, you should find a shop that specializes in road bikes. There should be several parked nearby that look as though they are currently in use.

Since you will be fully prepared to size yourself on a mountain or road bike, you won't be relying entirely on the shop to size you correctly. However, road bikes are so specific that you need a qualified person to measure your shoulder width, arm length, torso length, and stand over height. Otherwise you might very well end up with a road bike that doesn't fit or almost fits. Unless someone in the shop actually rides a road bike, don't plan to purchase one there. The shop may be a perfectly nice, reputable place but roadies are a breed apart, and it usually takes one to size one.

Let's talk about terminology. Do you want to ride on the road, off-road, technical single track, or cruise the neighborhood bike paths? Should you first take a peek at comfort bikes, mountain bikes or road bikes? Are you interested in hard tails, dual suspension, a really stiff road bike or just a fat soft seat? I'll provide a brief overview of what's actually on the bikes, but keep in mind that talking to a good sales person at a bike shop is way more fun than just simply reading a book about it, so go on over to your local bike shop to get the low down on what's really happening with bikes today. I'm just giving you a glimpse in this chapter.

Who needs gears, anyway?

Now that you have found your shop, you may have the usual questions and comments that many women (and men) ask at the door. For example, your first question could be, "Who needs 21 gears anyway?" With the added comment, "I just don't have time to learn all this new stuff, I just want a bike to ride to the gym and back." We in the bike business hear this every day, and these objections are all valid. Now to demystify. Shifting gears today is easy to learn and bike manufacturers have made it extremely simple to perform. Think of it this way, if you only had one gear on your car, your speed would remain the same and you'd never make it up hills. Gears are good.

The bike uses a derailleur system which means that the gears are shifted by means of little mechanisms (some people call them thingies) that move the chain sideways between differently sized cogs and chain rings. You select a low gear to go slowly uphill, a high gear to fast downhill, or an intermediate gear depending on the slope and type of the terrain in between. The bikes all have hand operated left and right brakes, front and rear derailleurs, two to three chain rings on the front and a number of cogs on the rear wheel. You really don't have 21-28 gears on your bike, you only have about six variations that you should be using.

The Secret: Here's the biggest tip you'll ever need to successfully shift gears when in doubt, combine only the smaller chain rings (front) with the larger cogs (rear) for easy pedaling, and the larger chain rings (front) with the smaller cogs (rear) for going fast down hills, and you'll be golden. Looking down at your chain while you are pedaling, always be sure it's straight. If it's at a diagonal angle, then your gear ratio isn't optimal.

Shifters generally appear on comfort bikes on the inside edge of the handlebar grips. To simplify conversation and avoid technical terms, I call these "Grip Shifters" after the company who first created them. Mountain bikes generally have top of the handlebar shifters that I call "Click Shifters," originally designed to click with each shift. Those of us who were around to change gears before clicking existed know that these are definitely improvements in bike technology. Specific details on shifting are included later in this chapter.

All brakes are not created equal

Comfort bikes and mountain bikes will be equipped with either what is knownas"V"brakesorthemorepriceybutplushdiscbrakes.Discbrakes arelikemotorcyclebrakesandifyoucanaffordthem,definitelygetthem. What a difference on the downhill! Road bikes are designed with tight cantilever brakes on the front and rear, combined with brake levers that double as shifters. These are extremely handy when you are suddenly faced with the need to shift and do not want to remove your hands from your handlebars to do it. All the brakes on newer bikes work extremely well, so remember, ease yourself into braking and always use your rear brake first to be on the safe side. Don't want to endo! More on this in a few minutes.

Prices

Our least favorite and most necessary topic. What you see is what you get in the bike world. But do you need it? Well, that depends. If you like really fabulously smooth shifting and braking and derailleurs that go snickety snick with a tiny click, you will be happiest with a bit more expensive components found on bikes over $700. If you are just looking for a bike to bomb around the neighborhood in and could care less if you have to click an extra click to get into the small chain ring from the middle chain ring, you'll be happy with the $400 to $650 range.

When talking about road bikes or full suspension mountain bikes, plan to spend between $1500 to $5000 to get the best you can get. A road bike with decent components can be had starting at $900, but I'd recommend spending $1500 for something a little better. Full suspension mountain bikes with a nice "gruppo" (group of components) will run you at least $2000, minimum. If you can't swing that for your road or full suspension mountain bike, wait till you save up enough money or catch something on sale that was originally in that price range.

Whatever you do, remember, do not, I repeat do not buy your bike from Wally's or any other Big Box store, because looks can be deceiving once you leave the sanctity of the bike shop. What looks like any other bike off the shelf can turn into something that falls apart and sits in your garage collecting expensive dust for what was supposed to be the better deal. You spent a hundred less at Wally's to save a buck rather than buy at the bike shop and now look what happened. After only two weeks of regular outings, you can't even ride the stupid thing because it doesn't work.

Ask your bike shop people to tell you more about such things as travel in suspension forks, and why one cross country full suspension bike is a shop favorite. Test ride as many bikes as possible to make an informed decision, and make sure that they are willing to switch out stems should you require a better fit which we'll discuss in another chapter. Have someone adjust your seat to ensure that it's level and not tilted. Get them to check your leg extension while you are pedaling and give you feedback for that final adjustment. You'll discover that by asking the right questions, and looking at the bikes themselves, there's a whole world out there in bike land that is fully accessible and attainable, right at your fingertips. If you are friendly to that surly mechanic and bring him a nice coffee sometime, he'll take good care of your bike for you when you need a quick fix. That guy with the tattoos and nose ring may tell you where he likes to ride his well-worn mountain bike. The tired looking sales woman with a weird bike glove tan line on her hands could belong to a nice group of women comprised of people just like you. How will you know what to expect until you get there?

Go get em Tiger!

The bike

Now that you've done the shop talk and got your bike all hooked up, and are obviously coming back to the shop for more accessories, you probably are still wondering about a few little details, such as how in the heck does this thing really work?

Let's take a moment to review the parts of your bicycle. You have the basic bike frame, the wheels, tires and skewers, the seat and seatpost, the brakes and levers, the derailleurs and shifters and all the cables in between. This package of fun will take you many miles to see many sights, as long as you remain safe and it continues to work properly. Before starting up for the day's ride, it may be a good idea to go over a few basics. There's a chapter on bike repair should you wish to be truly independent while out on your bike. I recommend learning how to tweak everything, but for now, we'll just talk about the basic mechanics.

Safety check

Wheels: Take a look at your wheel skewers' quick release levers. They are those things that attach your bike to the frame. Are they tight? You don't want your wheels to fall off on some great downhill pass, so double check the quick-release levers before each ride. The front lever should be flush with your bicycle's fork and the rear lever, which attaches to the rear dropouts, should be flush or pointing up. Never leave your levers loose or pointing down. To adjust and tighten, twist the thumbnut on the other end of the skewer while holding the lever until you can still fold the lever toward the hub. Fold it inward toward the bicycle. It should fit snugly against the fork and dropouts.

Handlebar stem: Stand in front of the bike, holding onto the front wheel with your legs. Try to twist the handlebars one way and then the other. Do they stay put, or is your stem bolt loose? Tighten the bolt with an Allen wrench if it is loose. The handlebars, like the skewers, should fit snugly in the headset.

Headset: Bounce the front wheel on the pavement. Do you sense or feel a rattle or vibration in the front end of the bike? If so, your headset may be loose. Hold the front brake lever tight, and try to roll the bike backwards and forwards. If the bike moves, it's most likely your headset. Adjusting a headset can be tricky. With the right tools and a good repair book you can do it yourself.

Hubs: If your bike's front end rattles, and it isn't the headset, your wheel hub may be loose. As with headsets, adjusting hubs is an exacting science that requires proper tools and a little bit of knowledge. You can do it if you want, or you can take your bike to the local bike shop for all of the adjustments I am describing here. Spin the wheels while observing their rotation through the brakes. Do you see a wobble, or is the wheel actually hitting a brake pad? Time to get that wheel trued, another exacting science requiring the proper tools and knowledge. While working in bike shops, I used their tools and taught myself how to true wheels with Jobst Brandt's *The Wheel Book* as a reference, and it was a long, slow process. If truing wheels is something you are truly interested in learning, never say never, because if I can learn how to do it, anyone can learn it.

While you are checking the wheels for wobble, pull the brake levers and see if the brake pads really hit the wheel rims, or if they actually hit the tire. You know what to do if they are off. Get out your tools. Call the shop.

Check the crankset/bottom bracket area for play. That's the thing your pedals are attached to, along with the bearing apparatus that allows the crank to spin. Grasp both crank arms, and pull them from side to side. Do you detect any play or vibration of any kind in the bottom bracket area? Does the crank creak when you are on the bike, pedaling uphill? Don't let it go, adjust it or get it adjusted before you ride. Read remarks above about truing wheels.

You are almost ready to ride. After a brief journey into the world of the derailleur, we will head out into the sunshine, helmeted, and with tires pumped up. First gears. Why are they here? What do they do?

Shifting gears

The single most confusing aspect of both mountain bikes and road bikes is the gearing system. Many women (and men) who are not familiar with the cycling world find themselves put off at the thought of riding a 21 or 27-speed bike. As I mentioned earlier, the bike doesn't really allow you to use all those gears. More than half of the possible combinations are not advisable, and you'll probably only use about six combinations in regular riding. The large range of gears is only there so the derailleur can easily move the chain from one spot to another, and each of the gears is useful in a certain combination. Just not all of them combine well with all of them.

I'll start at the beginning so you will become more confident about your bike's gearing system. Take a look at the handlebars. Follow the cable that begins at the shifter on the left side of the handlebar. This cable will lead to the front derailleur, located on the seat tube of the bike. The front derailleur's job is to move the chain from one chainring to the next. That is its entire reason for existence. Anytime you move the left shifter from one spot to the next, you move the chain with it. The left shifter moves your front chainrings, while the right shifter moves your rear cogs. The front derailleur moves the chain over two or three chainrings, which are located on the right hand crank. The reason why you need a front derailleur and two or three chainrings is simple: to ascend and descend at approximately the same cadence, or pedaling rate, measured in revolutions per minute.

Back to the handlebars. Follow the right shifter cable down to the back wheel, where it connects with the rear derailleur. This rear derailleur looks more complicated, and it is a bit larger than the front derailleur, but it does basically the same thing. The rear derailleur moves the chain between the cogs that are located on your rear wheel's hub. These cogs are combined into what is known as a cassette.

The chain must go over the derailleur pulleys at all times, which keeps the chain lined up properly with the front chainrings. If you shift the gears in either direction, you will move the derailleur up or down the cassette, from cog to cog. They will click into place if the bike is adjusted properly. It is indeed a satisfying click. As mentioned earlier, avoid combining large chainrings with large cogs, and vice versa, as your chain will get stretched and the whole gearing system can go out of whack. Plus you can break your rear derailleur as the pulley isn't meant to accommodate such a large amount of chain tension. Riding in the small chainring and the small cog is equally disastrous for a different reason. There is not enough chain tension to keep the rear derailleur taut, which means your chain can slip off into the space between your front crank and bottom bracket, taking you down hard onto the pavement as you suddenly spin out. Ouch!

Remember, small goes with large, and large goes with small in the world of front and rear derailleurs. The small chainring up front is your "granny" gear, and when you combine it with the large chainring in the back (also granny) you can climb just about anything. The large chainring on the front is your "hammer" gear, and when you combine it with the small chainring on the back you should definitely be going downhill fast.

My favorite hammer gear for off road is the "granny" in the rear (largest chainring) combined with the middle chainring in the front. It's sort of borderline as far as chain straightness, but it's close enough. I'll never forget watching my old friend Mel crank up some hard hills in Marin County California back in the early nineties. That's before she became a (no surprise) pro mountain bike racer. I'd just moved there from Oklahoma and I could not for the life of me get the strength in my legs to up something that steep in that gear, but I always wanted to be able to do it. I still try on occasion.

Braking

Be forewarned, brakes on newer bikes work extremely well. Start with applying gentle pressure to your right brake only. Unless you are a motorcyclist who has requested that the shop switch the brake levers to accommodate what you are used to on your motorcycle, the right lever controls your rear brake and the left lever controls your watch out for this one front brake. There's no such thing as anti-lock bike brakes, you can expect to plunge headfirst over your handlebars if you slam on the left brake for any reason. Another safe braking tip is to avoid braking while cornering, even if you end up getting concerned about your speed. Ride it out, and brake once you can straighten out your bike. If you have to brake while cornering, gently apply pressure to your right brake only, and just do it long enough to straighten your bike out before braking again.

Remember the safety check and do it every time you ride. Sometimes things happen to nice people and you don't want your brake pads to fall off, your handlebars to turn, your gears to slip or your wheel to be out of true while you ride. Before you test ride too far from the shop though, let's make sure your bike fits you perfectly.

6

The herstory of proper fit

"When I was a kid I used to pray every night for a new bicycle. Then I realized that the Lord doesn't work that way so I stole one and asked Him to forgive me."

—Emo Philips

Women used to have great difficulty finding a bike that fit right off the store room floor, because most mountain bikes and many road bikes were designed for men. In general, women have longer legs, a shorter torso, and shorter arms than men of the same size. Mountain bikes were once designed with long top tubes and long stems, which meant that the average woman would be stretched out beyond her comfort level on every mountain bike she tested.

These days, manufacturers realize the buying potential of women, and have taken care to create generic, off the shelf bicycles with a shorter, sometimes downward sloping top tube, shorter stem and shorter seat tube. The woman-friendly bike designs have even more features. Companies such as Specialized and Giant have created an entire line of women's specific models that also feature shorter handlebar width, shorter crank arms and smaller brake levers. It's not necessary to purchase only a woman's bicycle however, as the majority of women will be able to find a bike off the shelf that will fit them, providing you are willing to do your homework.

There are some tried and true rules a woman can follow to find the perfect fit. Knowing how to set up your own bike will increase your chances of a successful fit once you step into the bike shop. We'll begin with the easiest bike to fit, the mountain bike, then proceed to more complicated fitting required for a road bike. My advice is, purchase a tape measure with inches and centimeters. You'll need to measure bikes for yourself, and to assist the sales people, should they need it, in measuring your stand over height, leg length, arm length, and shoulder width. Before we get started, I'd like to say a few words about computerized fitting via the Body Scanner.

The Body Scanner is a tool that helps you and the sales people define exactly what type of riding you are most likely to engage in, and what type of bike is best for that riding style. It can be useful if you want a quick fit on your comfort bike, but it is not intended to perform fine tuning such as is needed for a road bike. I say this because I called up the Body Scanning tech support line and asked them specifically about the various uses of this machine. Being old school, I prefer to query the customer myself rather than use a gadget to record their information, punch in the numbers and use a print out to hand to the mechanic so he can use his Body Scanning tool to make the adjustments. I carry around an Alien tool in the shop with a tape measure and do all my own fitting adjustments for customers. I'm not saying you won't like the Body Scanning experience, I'm just saying it's not something I used while working at the bike shop, even though the owner wished I would. Now we'll talk about fitting your bike the old school way.

Comfort bikes, mountain bikes and road bikes frequently have sizes printed on the frame to give you an idea of how large or small the bike is before you sit on it. For example, some companies have XS, S, M, L and XL on their mountain bike frames. Other companies will print the sizes numerically, which can be a little confusing if you don't know that a size 18 bike means 18 inches from the center of the seat tube to the center of the crank, or from the top of the seat tube to the center of the crank, depending on how that individual company is measuring their bikes from which spot on the frame. What's a seat tube or a crank, right?

Bike companies measure frames using a highly unregulated and non-standardized measuring system that seems to change every year, but one thing is clear: You can whip out the old tape measure and follow the guidelines in this chapter to find the perfect fit, regardless of what size the bike frame has stamped on it.

Here's a tip: The seat tube length used to be directly proportional to how much stand over height you would have when straddling the bike. Now that many bikes are built with sloping top tubes, straddle height is still critical, but a seat tube length measurement may not be indicative of the bike size overall.

If you can straddle the bike, leaving at least two or more inches of crotch clearance between yourself and the top tube, the bike basically fits, height wise. Depending on what style of riding you are doing, you will need to also look at body extension and the degree of angle bend in your back.

Crucial to a good fit is that you are comfortable on the saddle, regardless of bike type. To ensure this, make the seat level by adjusting the seatpost clamp underneath it. Usually takes an Allen wrench. I generally push the seat all the way back and then slowly come forward before switching stems. You should be right in the middle of the seat, but the seat may be completely back on the post, or it may be in the middle. This is a fine tuning adjustment that always works. In case you have a bad seat, one that doesn't fit your body etc., you can try this first, then switch seats using the same technique. You'll find a good one that's right for you.

Comfort bikes

Comfort bikes are already built with an inherently upright rider position, meaning you can't stretch out on them to climb uphill. They have a fat saddle for a good reason, because you will really be using your sit bones on these bikes. There's just not much room to stand up and pedal, which would require leaning over on the bike when it's designed to keep you upright. Let's say you are 5'4 with a 30 inch inseam. Off the cuff, I'd say you'll ride a smallish comfort bike, but because your legs are long, you'll find that smallish comfort bike places you in such an upright position it's not comfortable. The medium comfort bike may be a little large for you, but the position is more comfortable because you have a slight bend in your back. If you want to bend over even more, let's say you are athletic and are looking for a bike to work out on, but thought you really needed to go with the most laid back and cozy looking ride you could find, consider checking out the recreational mountain bikes and putting a women's saddle on one.

Recreational mountain bikes

Depending on which company you are looking at, these bikes are built for comfort and some degree of versatility. The Giant Boulder is a classic example of a bike that can be used for working out and also for just cruising around the neighborhood. Even though at first glance it looks like a gnarly mountain bike, it's actually set up for a more upright but not too upright rider position. The frame angle is designed for a pretty laid back ride, but the rider can also stand up and pedal uphill without feeling like they are standing straight up.

Rider position is the fine line between comfort bikes and recreational mountain bikes, city cruisers, town bikes, etc. These days, bikes are built with the rider's intended use as the impetus for design.

What is primarily missing in the comfort bike, and somewhat missing in the recreational mountain bike, is the rider's ability to negotiate rough terrain. This is due to a non-aggressive riding position. These bikes are designed with long head tubes (where the handlebar stem is connected to the frame), which means that the handlebars are farther away from the wheel than a bike designed with shorter head tube. The farther away from the wheel, the less control the rider has over the bike. With comfort bikes, there is the additional distance added by the rider sitting upright with arms outstretched, rather than leaning forward with bent arms.

Performance is the trade off you make when purchasing bikes entirely for comfort, which is why I encourage some women riders to at least test ride non-comfort bikes once they are fitted with the proper stem and seat. A non-comfort bike can be quite comfortable with the correct adjustments, and it will out perform most varieties of comfort bike seen in shops today.

Mountain bikes

You can get as hardcore as you like with an aggressive mountain bike. Similar to a road bike design, the rider position on these babies is stretched out over the front wheel. You'll have more bend in your back and much more control over the bike in rough terrain. When sizing your bike off the shelf, jump on it and try to leap forward over the top tube while still straddling the bike. This is my ultimate quick fit test that always works in the shop. If you can't jump off the seat and onto the top tube without hurting yourself, then the bike is too big. Two inches of crotch clearance is required, ladies. This is also the test I use for kid bikes, because even though you might want junior to "grow into his bike," it just doesn't work once he tries the jumping over the top tube test. For your mountain bike, which I assume you will drop $500 or more to purchase, please review the rest of this chapter to learn how to adjust your seat properly and to decide if you may need a new stem.

Road bikes

Road bikes are sized using centimeters for more exact measurements. Today's off the shelf road bikes (meaning stock bicycles rather than specialized frames) generally will have some sort of sizing stamped onto them, but you will still need to fine tune your fit to dial it into perfection. The rules of fitting road bike frames are similar to fitting mountain bikes. You will need adequate crotch clearance and your intended riding style will dictate how stretched out over the bike is preferable.

Standover height

Standover height is easily measured by taking a contractor's square (metal L-shaped measuring device) and standing against a perfectly plumb, vertical wall. You hold one leg of the L between your legs, until it touches that most sensitive part, with the vertical leg of the L lying vertically down against the wall. Have someone measure from the top of the horizontal leg of the L to the floor and you will have your exact standover height. This measurement will make your initial search relatively simple, as you can measure each bike yourself from the top of the top tube to the floor and compare it with your standover height. It does help to wear the shoes you will wear to ride your bike. Give yourself at least 1.5 inches of clearance for the road bike, and 2-4 inches for the mountain bike.

More on sizing methods

Some bikes fit better than others. Why does one 18 inch mountain bike fit better than another 18 inch mountain bike? Or one Medium bike fit better than another Medium? Frankly I liked it better when all the companies at least measured numerically, because then the process of elimination was simpler. Today, as in yesterday, you'll discover that an 18 inch mountain bike may really have a 17 inch seat tube, measured from the top of the top tube to the center of the crank. The extended inch or so of extra seat tube found on some, not all, mountain bikes, will have no bearing whatsoever on the actual fit of your new bike, which is why some companies base their measurements from center to center. The following are some rough guestimates to give you an idea of what I'm talking about.

If you are approximately 5 foot 8 inches tall, you will most likely ride a 17.5 or an 18 inch mountain bike. The 17.5 bike may be measured from the top of the seat tube, making it really a 17 inch or a 16.5 inch bike. This bike will fit fine if you don't have extra long legs, like I do. If you have extra long legs, with a 34 inch inseam, you may need to buy the 18 inch bike, which is really a 17 or a 17.5-inch, depending on where it is measured. If the other manufacturer measures a 17-inch model from the top of the seat tube, adding an extra inch, you may think that since you ride an 18-inch in one, you should ride a 17-inch in another. Close enough right? Well, not exactly. The 17-inch model will actually be closer to a 16-inch if it has been measured from the top of the seat tube. This bike is too small for you.

How can you tell if a bike is too small or too large? First, know your standover height. Then, straddle the bike that seems closest to your physique. If you have a couple of inches to spare, you can at least presume the bike is not too large. However, if you feel incredibly crunched up when you test ride it, unless the stem is really short, you may need to test ride a bike by another manufacturer. Bicycles are rarely unavailable in all sizes, but the shop may be low on a certain size because they had a busy weekend or you may be one of those in between people who are going to almost, but not quite, fit on two different sizes.

An example of this sizing problem is a woman who is 5 foot 8 with a 30-inch inseam, or a woman who is 5 foot 6 with a 32-inch inseam. Both women will fit either a 17-inch or an 18-inch mountain bike if they have an average torso length for their height. Since a 16-inch mountain bike is usually more like a 15-inch, I don't recommend that size for anyone over 5 foot 5 unless she has an inseam of 29-inches or less.

The 5 foot 8 woman will not have much crotch clearance on an 18-inch mountain bike, and feel crunched up on the 17-inch bike, which will allow for plenty of clearance but not enough top tube length to accommodate her long torso. The 5 foot 6 woman will comfortably straddle the 17-inch bike, but will need quite a bit of seatpost showing to accommodate her extra long legs.

Rules to remember

I know, rules right? But there are a few and if you follow them your fit situation will improve dramatically. Level the seat before doing anything else. Move the seat all the way back then slowly work it forward to get the perfect fit. You need at least two inches of crotch clearance from the top tube to comfortably ride your mountain bike off road. The mountain bike allows you to use various hand positions, which are different than those used with a road bike. Road bikes require less crotch clearance, but you still need to be able to jump off the bike onto the top tube without hurting yourself, so one and a half inches is a good place to start. You will be locked onto your road bike for longer periods of time so the fit should be absolutely perfect.

Stem and brakes

We've discussed stem and brakes a bit, so let's take it one step further. Your stem should have a slight rise, unless you ride some kind of sick downhill or hardcore racing road bike, in which case you will have a negative rise in your stem. The really hardcore could care less about pain, and need that kind of negative rise to get the most performance possible from their bikes, but we'll stick to those of us who are into performance with only a little pain, rather than performance with a lot of pain. LOL!

As I was saying, you should not feel too crunched up or stretched out when grasping the handlebars. Your handlebars, on a road bike, should be fairly close to your shoulder length. On a mountain bike, you may find initially that wider handlebars make the bike easier to handle. Eventually, narrower handlebars that accommodate your shoulder width will be the most efficient with optimal performance. Kind of like a surfboard, the big long fatties will allow you to stand up and surf little breaks, but the smaller guns make the wave your playground.

When you grasp the brake levers on your mountain bike, they should fit nicely into your hands without undue stretching on your part. If they do not, have the shop adjust the brake levers on the handlebars. There's a little hex screw that turns in using a number 2 metric Allen wrench if you want to do it yourself. This will shorten the distance required to brake the bike if you have smaller hands or shorter fingers.

Saddle

Your saddle is everything and again, it should be exactly level. While riding you should not be seated toward the rear of the saddle, nor on the tip. I see people (usually guys, no offense intended!) riding their bikes all the time with their saddles tilted up to the extreme or tilted down to the extreme. This is not a good fit but they are used to it. I suggest you find a comfy (not huge, fat or overly cushioned) saddle that is designed for fit women riders. Search until you find the right one for you and work with a shop who understands the importance of a perfect saddle. These babies are simple to remove from the seatpost and if the saddle doesn't work right, trust me, nothing else will either.

Seatpost position

When first adjusting your seatpost length, find a position that will allow you to sit with your leg almost fully extended, with a slight bend in the knee, while riding. To find this adjustment, first place your foot on the pedal with the ball of your foot exactly flat, while the pedal is horizontal. Place a plumb line at the bony protrusion located at the bottom of your knee cap and the top of your shin bone. When dropped, it should directly intersect with the center of the pedal spindle. Adjust the saddle either forward or backward to achieve this line. If your seatpost is too extended, your hips will rock from side to side when you pedal. If your seatpost is not extended enough, your knees will have more bend, which can cause muscle strain and other problems.

Ideal position

The ideal position places your body at a 90-degree angle when measured with arms locked. Some women like to sit more upright, while others want to be more stretched out. As mentioned earlier, these variations in rider position will directly affect your ability to negotiate paths, trails, roads and bumps with your bike. The 90-degree angle is optimal for performance. This means that while you are seated and riding the bike, your arms are at 45 degrees, and your legs are at 45 degrees.

If you prefer to initially ride in a more upright position, remember that you sacrifice climbing efficiency and offer greater wind resistance which will lead to earlier fatigue. You can always change your stem as your riding ability improves, thus achieving the preferred 90-degree angle at a later date. Please note: this only applies to road and mountain bikes, as the comfort bike is not designed to accommodate a rider position of 90-degrees.

Pedals

I personally can't use clipless pedals due to an ankle injury, but if you can manage them, they are very helpful for road bikes. Clipless pedals do not come with traditional toeclips, and require special shoes to "click" into the pedal. Find pedals that allow for "float," as most do these days. This will enable your feet to move around horizontally upon the pedal without wrenching your knees. Try to keep your feet as close together as possible. This means you need to find a crank set, pedals and shoes that do not place your feet too far apart. If you are used to wearing high heels, you can either relearn how to place your foot horizontally on the pedal, or have the bike adjusted to accommodate your different stride. Mountain bikes do great with both clipless and BMX platform pedals, and comfort bikes generally are fine with the flat pedals that are already installed on the bike. The trusty toe clip pedal is still available for those who want to strap onto their pedals.

I hope this chapter has helped you understand the mechanics of fit as they apply to your riding style. There's so much more we could discuss here, but I'm ready to start accessorizing my bike. Let's talk about GEAR!

Could you resist skipping work to ride with these two?

TREK

The Bob trailer. I haul veggies from my garden in the summer to our local bar so the owner and manager can have some freshies.

She's already won the race in her heart.

Cool happy chicks I met at Kendafest. Note the bumps and bruises, those were probably from riding, don't ya think?

Someone said this, “You are only as old as your spine.”

Yahtzee

This fine lady was working at The Downtube in Albany when I stopped by to take some photos. She's posing with her customized ride, which also doubles as her car. Note the proud, happy look on her face. This is what cycling is all about, you and your pet bike.

Sometimes I think that girl's bikes just want to have fun. And what's wrong with a little fun? These ladies' recreational "comfort" bikes are designed for a very upright position when you ride them with a large, comfy seat for your tush. If you are looking for speed and hill climbing, you'll need to look elsewhere as these babies are designed for your comfort first and foremost. Think about this, is your favorite ride a mellow cruise through town to the local icecream shop (do we have those anymore?) where you sit with your friends and have a nice cone? If so, this bike is for you. Take it easy, take it nice and slow, and hang out for hours cruising around on your comfort machine. That's right, it's time to relax, and you can actually do it on a bike.

These puppies are designed to get you down that trail in style, with less hard knocks, and a fast thrill. The little seat should clue you in, full suspension cross country mountain bikes are only for the gnarly. You won't be sitting down very much.

MARLIN DISC

Plaines in Pittfield knows how to put on a good bike showcase. From their website: Plaine's was opened by Mitch Plaine, its owner, when he was 21 years old. Our master mechanic, Mike, has been with us for over 30 years, and he can fix everything but a broken heart. Claudia, our manager, takes care of the day to day things, she and Mike compliment each other nicely.Opened in 1974 on the corner of West Housatonic and South St. in Pittsfield, the original merchandise were just bicycles and service; but we evolved to start including Cross-Country skis. 15 years later, we found a large colonial down the street, completely gutted it, and set up shop where we are today. With now double the size from our previous store, we added Alpine skis to our merchandise, and eventually Snowboards, Snowshoes, and everything else.

FINANCING
AVAILABLE
NO PAYMENTS
NO INTEREST FOR
ONE YEAR
SPECIALIZED
SPECIALIZED

FINANCING
AVAILABLE
NO PAYMENTS
NO INTEREST FOR
ONE YEAR
SPECIALIZED
TEST BIKE
TEST CENTER
SPECIALIZED
SPECIALIZED

If you are ever in the neighborhood, stop by and visit three of my favorite East Coast shops: The Mountain Goat, in Williamstown; Berkshire Outfitters in Adams; and The Downtube in Albany.

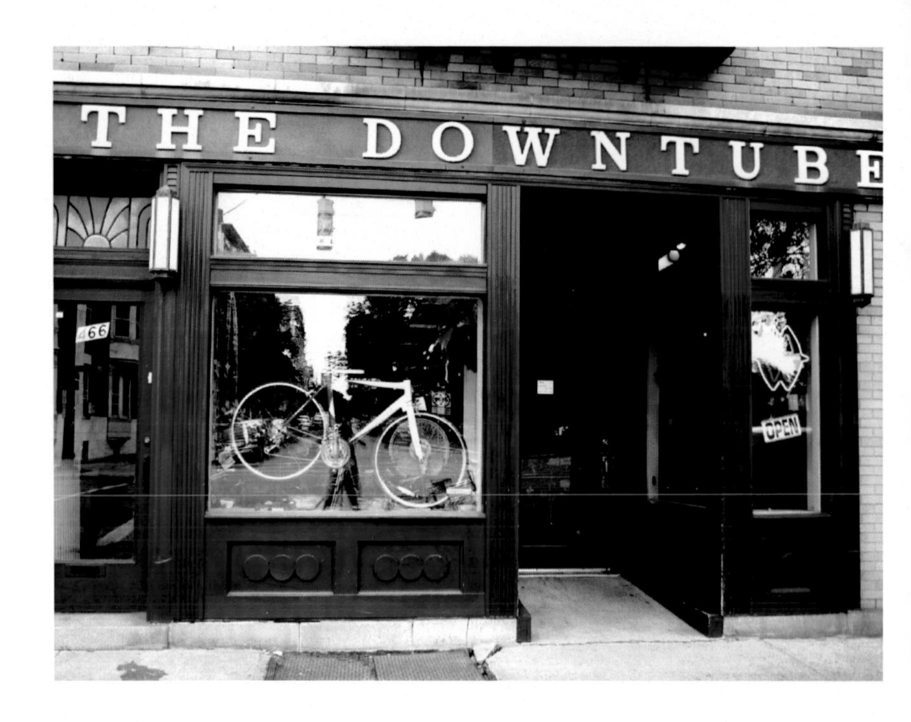
THE DOWNTUBE
466
OPEN

SMITH

I have a whole story devoted to The Spoke in Williamstown, and I really can't say enough about Paul, the owner. He's the coolest, the best and the smartest bike guy I know. As for bike trivia, Paul should be on Jeopardy. And this lady Barb, well she rides so many miles that she should be helping Paul with that bike. In fact, if I recall she was telling him the pros and cons of the flat handlebar bike compared to her old favorite dropped handlebar road bike. Wonder which one she finally decided is best for touring...I'm voting for the old favorite road bike. This bike seems like it would be optimal for town riding, and city commuting due to the flat handlebars. Should you be in the Berkshires, visit The Spoke and check out their crazy mechanic shop. Look for the dude with the nose ring and take him a latte for me. Microbrew beer is always appreciated too, FYI. They might even offer to ride with you.

OUNTAIN BIKES

Wouldn't you love to step into a beautiful shop and be greeted by a friendly lady at the counter, waiting to help you find your dream bike? Then there's the backroom. Granted, the two mechanic shops look totally different. I can tell you from experience that the same quality work comes out of both of them. It's a beautiful thing when you can take a broken bike and put it back together again. Having the right tools, or a shop where there are guys with the right tools, or even better yet, a shop with there are women with the right tools is the only way to go. I'm quite fortunate to have so many great shops in our area, but there's only one shop where I can put my bike on the stand and work on it if I'm truly in need of some tutoring, and that's at The Spoke. We all have to have our homie shop. Would a little mess scare you away? Think again my friend. These guys know where every tool is located, and if they let you touch their tools, well, you are golden.

Clothes and bling. Accessories. Nuff said.

Just a quick comment about food...if you want to ride like this, you have to eat more than 1200 calories a day. Go ahead, chow down, then put the hammer on and ride. Oh, and here's a tidbit from my days riding with Barry and Gravy and Gail in Marin County. Never turn down food that is offered to you on the trail. Ever.

Those of us who have had the pleasure of riding with Inge call her the Queen of Gnarl. She puts the hurt on all the boys and smiles while she's doing it. Luckily for me, I got her into longboarding in Washington Park, Albany, where we are more or less equals.

TRIPS FOR KIDS
MARIN
TREK

KID
GIANT

Here are happy new mechanics in action, proud to be a part of Trips for Kids in Marin County, California. Thank you Marilyn, for starting such a great organization. You have made a difference in many children's lives.

Ya'll come back now!

7

Accessories

"All bicycles weigh fifty pounds. A thirty-pound bicycle needs a twenty-pound lock. A forty-pound bicycle needs a ten-pound lock. A fifty-pound bicycle doesn't need a lock."

—Anonymous

Ladies, the single most important accessory you can buy for your bike riding experience will muss up your hair, totally. That's a helmet if you haven't figured it out yet. Your head is where everything is stored, including fine motor skills and the ability to feed yourself, read a book, do your corporate job downtown and enjoy the sight of your lovely daughter as she walks rolls rides across the room. Okay?

Helmets

Find a helmet that fits comfortably and that you can stand to wear. You will need to put it on your head each and every time you take your bike for a ride. The bike helmet can double as a roller blade and longboard helmet, so keep it handy at all times and wear it every time you do anything that could possibly including banging your head against something hard. Even if you only bang your head once in a lifetime (and if you engage in adventure sports I promise you'll bang it more frequently) you should be wearing something to cushion your brain cells from impact. Get a lightweight hat or baklava to fit under your helmet when it's cold.

Hydration

The next thing you should purchase for yourself is a good container for your water supply. I personally favor Camelbaks as they hold a lot of water and force you to pretty much continually drink and therefore remain hydrated. You can also store your stuff in your Camelbak, including food keys and cell phone. A lot of people opt for less expensive water bottles, but if you take into account the motion of reaching down every time to disengage the bottle from the bike, you'll see that it's safer by far to just carry the thing on your back while you ride and take little sips from the twisty loopy thing that delivers water to your thirsty lips. You can keep them clean by adding a little grapefruit seed extract to the water and putting a large spoon in the empty bladder when it's not in use.

Camelbaks are a great invention. I used to watch people in Oklahoma with their water supplies strapped to their backs, while I had three water bottles on my bike, and think to myself, no way I'd ever be caught in public wearing that silly thing. This was in the eighties and it was freaking hot in Oklahoma back then. Still is I hear. That was before I moved to California and ran out of water on a long ride day with a bunch of guys in Palo Alto.

I got totally dehydrated and had to drink super-suspiciously murky creek water after dumping a full load of iodine into it as I really didn't want to get sick from the various parasites and contaminants that surely were swimming around in it. I looked specifically for water with living things like tadpoles to ensure it wasn't nuclear waste or other chemically deadened water. After I drank some big gulps out of that creek I permanently borrowed my then husband's Camelbak and never used a water bottle again. Yech. That was truly gross water in Palo Alto. Don't be me, get yourself a good solid water supply system before you are faced with a similar circumstance.

Shoes

The next thing you really need to get is a toss up between bike gloves and bike shoes, but I'll say get the shoes first if you are strapped for cash. You can use regular hiking shoes, trail shoes or lightweight hiking boots, depending on the terrain and what time of year it is. Keene sandals do a fantastic job in the summer, they have a stiff sole and a wide foot bed with protected toes, so you can mountain bike in them at will with no discomfort. This is assuming you have BMX pedals on your bike, which I highly recommend, now that I am in the recommending mode. You can go clipless too, but you'll need to purchase the shoes and you won't have the flexibility you have with BMX pedals. On a road bike, I'd definitely get clipless pedals and invest in the roadie shoes. They will cost you between $100 and $180 for the shoes you want. Don't worry, it's a lot of money but they'll last you for a long time.

Gloves

After dumping some cash on the above, you need to get some gloves. They are cheap, only about $20 to $30, and will save the ulnar nerves in your hands from permanent damage. Just get some gloves with padding in the appropriate spots. I've seen gloves on the market that don't really have any padding; I kind of wonder what the people who manufacture these are thinking. Anyway, you can find some with padding, just try them on till you find some that fit well and work with your style. Get long fingered gloves for winter, short for summer. Two sets.

Shorts

Bike shorts cost between $50 and $100 plus. If you ride much at all, you'll need them unless you just enjoy pain. They feel like a diaper and are awful, absolutely awful to hang out in and drink coffee but they are fabulous while you are riding your bike. They make the whole experience fairly pain free for the length of time you are riding. Just like a soft squishy foam mattress on bikes. Get the women's specific if you can find them as the seams are in a different place than on the men's. You'll see what I mean once you wear them around on your bike.

I hate bike shorts so much that I leave regular clothes in the car and strip those damp stank suckers off as soon as I am done riding my bike, before I go home if I've driven even a few miles because I cannot stand to wear them one millisecond longer than necessary. Most women don't hang out in their bike shorts. That said, you should know I own four pairs, and I hate all of them with an equal passion. I hate Black Bottoms especially which is why that's the only shorts I'll buy. They last forever and fit perfectly.

Cyclometers

Ah, now we are getting into the gear. Get yourself a good cyclometer that measures cadence. That's around $60 and well worth it, especially on a road bike. You can focus on your training, get your cadence up to a decent level and improve your performance pretty quickly. Don't let the average mileage get you down if you notice you are only going about 13 mph. Did you stop and leave the computer running? Did you climb a bunch of hills? Look at your total miles, your top speed and the time elapsed. That's what the cyclometer is all about. Cateye is a great company that makes a premiere product, and they back their goods.

Carrying stuff

Under the seat bags are necessary for small stuff, like some cash and tools. They are inexpensive. Should you wish to carry a lot of stuff, such as in a commute situation, I'd recommend you purchase a solid Blackburn rack for your bike. They cost around $60. You can strap your laptop on it and cruise downtown in style, not worrying about carrying it. Blackburn has been around for a long time and their stuff is totally bombproof. A Timbuk2 messenger bag is another way to carry your stuff. I have three of those and have used them for my commute over the San Francisco bridge and from my bike shop jobs in the Haight. Great gear, cost from $60 to $200. You'll notice none of this stuff is cheap, however you can take it from me, if you spend more now you'll have the gear that works later, when you need it the most. This stuff lasts forever and works really well. They invented the messenger bag for messengers in California. Most bike accessories grew out of the need for the item, and people actually used it multiple times, then marketed it.

If you really want to travel, get some panniers and/or a Bob trailer. Cost around $250 for either or. Good panniers are worth every penny, although I prefer the Bob over panniers for longer distances. That's just me, as others who are also experienced prefer panniers. If you are traveling any distance, get the good gear because you want it to carry you all the way there and back.

Fashion

Next on the list is looking for that perfect jersey. Well you can look for it or you can leave it. I like Shebeast, they have some really cool jerseys for women. Or you can just put on a cotton tank top for the summer, and get a tan. For winter, I wear Italian wool jerseys, with tights and warm socks. Burley still makes the premiere rain gear as they are out of the northwest where it's wet more than it's dry. I use my New England winter under gear for bike under gear when the riding gets cold and yes, I look kind of funny but quite frankly as Scarlett said you know the rest.

Lights

You can shop for gear all day long. Find a blinking rear light for your bike if you are out at dusk and after. Find a really bright front lamp, such as one by NiteRider, if you are out at dark. We are talking 32 watts and a rechargeable battery. Let the cars think you are a motorcycle. They will get out of your way sooner and you'll be safer. The blinking red light in the rear kind of looks like the cops, which is a good thing. Hey, get two. They are cheap. I'll cover tools in the repair section but a brief run down of the basic necessities to carry on the bike, if you don't want to read about repairs, is as follows:

Tools

Get a pump that fits into your Camelbak. I never strap a pump onto my bike frame, what a hassle. I just take one along for everything, as I have multiple bikes. Besides, pumps get muddy and none of my bikes like to have anything strapped to them anyway. They all told me so. Have a Topeak Alien tool in your bike bag at all times. That's the single best multi tool on the market and has been ever since they introduced it in the nineties. Yes, I'm opinionated. Those Aliens cost around $35 to $45 and they will last you for a decade or longer. I still have my original and use it all the time. They are easy to use and have everything on them that you could need on your bike. Just go buy one. Don't settle for anything but a Topeak Alien. No they didn't pay me to write this, that's the same tool I still carry today and I'll swear by it.

If I haven't convinced you to get an Alien, then purchase a metric Allen set with size 2 to 8 mm wrenches, a spoke wrench, tire levers, a chain breaker, a Phillips screwdriver and some box wrenches. Everything is metric on a bike, and everything can come up standard on a skateboard. Go figure. I haven't figured that one out myself. Anyway, the tool combination I just described will cost you more and take up more space and weigh more than just getting the Alien multi tool but you need the full load for basic repair should your bike not work right once you are out the gate.

Add a Presta adaptor to your arsenal. That's to make the skinny valve on the tire tube fit the fatter pump that's meant for the fatter Shraeder valve. These adaptors cost $2 and will make that gas station pump fit your tube. Try not to blow the tube up if you have to use the adaptor at the gas station. I once found myself in the pouring rain after a 40 mile jaunt with a blown pump and a blown tube and a Presta adaptor. I was in the middle of nowhere getting freezing cold fast and I came up to a farmhouse. I sort of hobbled in my bike shoes with my non-working flat Masi 3V Volumetrica road bike which under normal conditions is a real peach but this day it was totally non-working and dead, anyway, I hobbled with my broken bike to the farmhouse. Inside the farmhouse shop, the farmers kept a compressor. Ah, and I had my handy dandy $2 Presta adaptor. I screwed it onto my newly installed tube, which I had installed in the pouring rain after flipping the tire off then back on, then blown the pump, and it worked beautifully.

Fully aired up, I thanked the friendly farmers and madly pedaled off through the freezing pouring rain to my final destination, a Berkshire legendary Five Corners cup of hot java and a cookie, and my parked truck with warm dry clothing. My male riding buddy was waiting for me, comfortably sucking down some hot java himself. He had a working pump but hadn't noticed I'd flatted a few miles back so he'd pedaled on to our agreed upon snack spot and the end of the road that day. See many mishaps in "Riding with the Guys." Story of my life.

Flats

You still need to have spare inner tubes and tire irons. Keep them around even if you never have a flat. You should know, there's a whole bikie superstition around flats—never say you never have flats. Always use *yes they are heavier but so what* Specialized Armadillo road tires and you never will have flats. I didn't say that, besides I can't really say which are the best mountain bike tires to avoid flats. We used to have to use tire liners in Oklahoma because of the goathead thorns, monsters with spikes, and tire liners are considered really heavy. Probably the Specialized Armadillos will work best on mountain bikes too. If they want to send me some I'll try them out. I'd say use anything with Kevlar. Women alone with their flats puts us into the vulnerable position of not being able to continue riding our bikes. If you grow up where I did, in Lawton, Oklahoma, having a flat in many areas of town means having to deal with a small crowd of "well meaning" guys stopping by to "help," with not so good intentions. Get the good stuff, ladies. You'll be glad you did.

Major surgery

Look at it this way, if you have a full load of tools and some extra tools and vitamin I if someone hurts herself, you can always help out a fellow cyclist in need. The good karma of sharing your tools and tubes and lubes will return to you indeed. I've seen people repair blown out tires with Power Bar wrappers, Duct tape and forest grass way out in the boonies in California, so take some Power Bars and Duct tape just to be safe. Throw in a few Cliff bars too, they taste good even after all these years and those wrappers are pretty tough. You just never know when disaster might strike and it's best to have the readily available repair parts in your bag. There is all kinds of other stuff you can buy for your bike but we are talking about bells and whistles that is subject to your personal preference. The aforementioned gear is the primary load you'll need for comfort and essentials on the road and trail.

As possibly the only woman rider in your group, rather than get stereotyped as the helpless female, you'll want to be prepared. I hope you have your helmet on, your light battery recharged, your Camelbak full and you've already had a pee break, because there's no turning back now. You are riding with the guys and it's gonna be a long, gnarly trip till you get back home, my dear. Could be after dark of the next day of the week. You'll miss work.

8

Riding with the guys

"The bicycle is just as good company as most husbands and, when it gets old and shabby, a woman can dispose of it and get a new one without shocking the entire community."

—Ann Strong, Minneapolis Tribune, 1895

A day in the life of the Spoke

Dude, it's like I was suddenly knee-deep in mud, watching the gyrating, neon rear ends of my new pals cruise away. Here I was, stuck behind some guy named Big Al on a killer Serotta who basically stopped mid-crank with a mud puddle at his right, did a dirt track stand long enough for me to dab, big time, then took off. Silly me, I figured he'd keep going past the mud, but no, he had to take a breather. I took a dive, and here I am, not pedaling. My hands and knees are black with thick, viscous, Massachusetts mud, and it's wicked cold outside.

"Hey, wait up," I call out, quickly deciding that to gripe would not be cool, especially on my first ride with these guys who work at the Spoke bike shop in Williamstown. I showed up, ready to ride, and hung out for hours while the guys did their thing—finally, we were off to some trail in Vermont called White Oaks. What's a little mud to a dude woman like myself who loves to ride with men like these on a crisp, March evening during my first spring in nearby upstate New York? We're right on the MA/NY/VT border, which means tri-state rides everyday.

I think I better catch them before they totally leave me in this puddle. I put the pedal down and sprint through the field, pass into forest, then uphill to the max. There they are, right ahead. Hoping they'll chill, I breathe harder and pedal faster. Shift down into granny/middle chainring and hope I can hold it. Nope. Granny/little chainring—kachink! Love that shortcage XT rear derailleur. "What's up?" I ask. No reply. "Dudes, did you see that mud hole back there?" They look at me, then shrugged.

"Don't get your wheel too close behind Big Al," Dave cautions. "He rides kinda funny." Al nods in agreement. I notice some serious road rash on Dave's hip. "Take a fall yourself, dude?" He cracks up. Billy holds up the videocam, and they exchange expressions like, is this chick for real?

"Due, no dude, I always look like this," Dave retorts. "Cancha see my handlebar's bent?" Oh. He really took a big one. His worn-out, faded yellow Yokota looks like it, too. My little escapade becomes less important. Dave supposedly never crashes, they say. "I was trying' to jump that stump over there," he gestures toward some mondo fallen tree. "Almost made it, but that branch got my bottom bracket." Very cool, I think to myself.

"We off?" Billy asks me. He sits astride his worn out, size large, black Yokota. "We waited, yuh know." Back on the faithful steeds, we pedal uphill further. Pretty soon, we're cruising up some big rocks in a river bed. I'm walking by this time, straining to keep up. Billy hands off the videocam to Dave, then attempts to catch serious air over a jump. Dave films the whole thing as Billy flies through the air, and lands with a loud thump on the other side. I slowly ride over the bump, and land very softly on the muddy trail. They snicker, but I realize that they aren't snickering at me, it's some private joke. In fact, they are real gentlemen, and I decide to start hanging out with them, cos they actually like each other. Back at the bike shop/hacienda, Al congratulates me on my good humor after the mud-soaking as I ruefully scrape some kind of brown, goopy, suspicious-smelling crap off my shoes. Dave said to me later on after we rode many rides together, "If you ride, you're cool." Plus he started giving me deals on Powerbars which really sucked me in.

Paul Rhineheart, the Spoke's owner, is no slouch at riding bikes himself. He can often be spotted trying to put a dent in the latest mountain bike line he is thinking of selling before he'll display it in the shop. After all, if Paul can break it, so can you. Usually, he doesn't break the bike because they are picky about new lines and generally stick to Diamondback and Jamis, along with a few others. (They finally trashed the Yokotas, but it took years of hammering.) Paul, Dave, Billy and Andy, who's been too busy lately to ride with us, make up the core group of guys who work at the Spoke. They ride, eat, and drink beer together.

There are always a few women wrenching at the Spoke, depending on who's in college this semester, and who's racing. If Dave or Billy are working, you can talk about everything from the mountain bike industry standards in Marin County, California, to what's happening in European road racing. It's a truly casual place. Nine Inch Nails, Nirvana, Alice In Chains, Pearl Jam fill the shop's airways as customers lounge about yakking about local races, the best beer breweries, and pizza.

I heard we were gonna do another fifty miler road bike ride up the Mohawk Trail on Route 2 past North Adams.... last time we did that, Big Al crashed into an embankment and burned, bending his front wheel. This time, I had enough room to avoid wobbling Al when he first began to shudder. The spectacular crash and burn happened when he lost control of his handlebars, hit the embankment, then flipped upside down, his Trek 2300 literally flying through the air. Billy took the trashed wheel off its crooked aluminum fork, gleefully banged it repeatedly on the pavement, then reattached it to Al's bike. It looked like it was in true. "Damn, you're good," I comment to Billy the wildman. He laughs. I laugh too as we climb into the saddle and laboriously begin our thirty-five mile mostly uphill ride back home to Williamstown.

Is it really like that to ride with the boys?

Yes.

The above description could be your typical ride with the guys if you want to go where they go, and do what they do. It's not always easy hanging with the boys but the rewards are great, and I have discovered that they really do enjoy having female company on their rides. That's right ladies, they like having us along. I know because I have asked on many occasions and always received a resounding yes, please, come ride with us.

How to hang with the guys, that is the question. Well, first of all, remember that being in the kind of shape that the guys are in sometimes means you need to train a little first before trying to hang on their harder rides. Ask what type of ride it's going to be before joining up. Even though they want us along, that doesn't mean they want to wait for us continually to catch up.

I showed up at the Spoke that fateful day with a road bike and a mountain bike, because that's what they said to do. There wasn't a definitely planned ride in the works yet, so I had to go with their flow, not my own. Riding with the guys means letting them decide what they want to do and joining in with their fun, cheering when they do stupid stuff like jump over logs fly through the air and crash intentionally, and also fixing their bikes when they break down. Oh maybe that's why they like having me along, I always take tools, hmmm.

Seriously, hanging with the guys will increase your strength and make your hardness factor harder. They don't whine much, and they generally push themselves like machines. Back in California I used to hang with these guys who basically told me to be ready for a 10 hour plus mountain bike ride. I never knew where we were going, only that it would be a long ride and that I wouldn't be able to find my way out alone after a certain point. We took food, money, lights, clothing, lots of water, and were prepared to go until they decided it was over. My main riding buddy Barry London had calves the size of my thighs. I knew that he meant business when he said it would be a long ride that day. Collapse the calendar, put away the cell phone and plan to be out of touch for a good long while. Your bike better work well and you should be prepared for anything and everything cos riding with these guys was the ultimate test of your endurance. We are talking about Marin County California in the early nineties, back when most of West Marin was off limits to mountain bikes, forcing us to play cat and mouse with rangers to get in our daily rides.

Scary night rides

I'll never forget my first night ride on Mt Tam. I had on my road bike shoes as I'd ridden my road bike to a friend's house in Mill Valley. We called her Penn Monster. Her husband, Arne, was an electrical genius and built Tesla coils in his living room. I showed up at Penn and Arne's house and they informed me after some chocolate chip cookies that we were going on a night ride. They handed me a fully equipped mountain bike with dropped handlebars and a light and off we went. I recall being fairly tweaked as we negotiated a twisty windy trail that had 500 foot drop offs and tree roots galore. One false move and you are off the bike, down the ravine, in pitch black night. I focused on the dimly lit trail ahead, put my fear on temporary hold and rode carefully, following the mighty Penn Monster as she ripped and roared down the trails with Arne behind her. These were the days of Gravy and Caroline, Gail, Barry and myself, and many others who also cruised the trails with us at night. You see, we were forced to hide at night in the darkness and only occasionally use the lights when totally desperate in the trees to get from point A to point B, both legal trails. The off limits part could be a short 100 yard link between the two. Silly huh?

My night vision became extraordinary back then. Riding with the guys meant riding with their girlfriends and wives, who inspired me for the rest of my life. The guys know how to have fun and the girls know how to keep the fun flowing. The girls are the ones who pack the extra water, extra food and some M and Ms to keep us moving. The guys are the ones who also remember to slow it down once in a while and make sure so and so catches up. Every now and then, we'll get into a serious groove and the guys girls thing just goes away as we all chase the same little rat that's gnawing at us, making us get out there and ride in drizzle and freezing rain, muddy hillsides and cold, dark nights. The rat makes us all crave our spinning wheels and hurtles us towards the next beyond the next trail. Ah, just one more trail before we go home. That's us. How did I become one of us? That's another story.

Spinning

Learning to spin is crucial. If you learn to spin you can ride all day long. It's simple really, using your gears. Think of a standard transmission car, or if you are like me, remember your motorcycle days. Use your bicycle gears as if you were in a car or a motorcycle and you'll find yourself spinning the same rpms no matter what level of ground you are going up and down. Spinning and using your gears are the most important skills to learn if you want to save your energy for the last thirty miles of your ride and also save your knees for the next sixty years of your life.

Now that you are practicing riding your bike in the winter, spend some time daydreaming about great rides you've had and hook yourself up to a bike trainer. Here's an idea: Okay, it's snowing outside and you live in flat USA where skiing isn't possible. You are on your trainer but you are bored stiff because there's just no challenge in shifting gears unless you actually have some terrain and let's face it, the basement still looks the same. You can think about other things while you ride, or, you can plug in your favorite Scrubs and Sex in the City reruns and spin for a show or two. Before you know it, you'll be dripping in sweat and won't even notice that you worked out. Hey, I like that idea so much that maybe I'll go downstairs myself and work off some of this fresh baked bread and Parmesan cheese I just pigged out on. Actually if you want to know the truth, I can't stand spinning in the basement and I'll go outside or sit around and do nothing any day rather than spinning in the basement. But, with four llamas, a goat, three dogs and a cat, there's not alot of time to spend sitting around so maybe I'll force myself against my will to get off my rear end and just do something.

Then there was road riding

While you are down there spinning on your road bike, remember that hanging in a pack is about staying on someone's rear wheel, also politely known as drafting. Well, we have another term for drafting and it's less polite.

Sucking wind is something that must be carefully performed as it's a fine art that requires finesse. You have to trust your fellow riders enough to get about five inches from their rear wheel doing up to 35 miles per hour, I kid you not. Let's say that happens, and you are in a tight pack and that person's rear wheel that you've been sucking suddenly wobbles. Well, you'll fall down and several riders behind you in the pack will have to either ride over your prostrated and bleeding body or wreck their bikes. Which would you choose? I know what I'd do, bunny hop you if I could! This has happened to me, bottom line, learn to draft and never let your bike wobble if you don't want your fellow pack mate to fall down. Because once you cause a wreck, the pack will not allow you back in again, period. To ride with the guys, you have to share the code of honor which requires you to never, ever make someone else wreck. If you are unsure of your skills, hang at the back of the pack and slowly learn as you go. Envision not wobbling. Watch out for that fellow's rear wheel, I think it's about to wobble. Watch their brake hands to see if they are about to hit their brakes because once they do, their bike will wobble and you, my dear, have the potential to go down.

Hill climbing for fun

If you really want to learn to climb hills, you have to get out there and do it, over and over. I personally like to stand up and climb, but some people prefer to sit down and climb. It's a personal preference. I have noticed that allowing my body weight to turn the pedals rather than using my thigh muscles while sitting hurts less, but that could be different for you.

Climbing can be fun, I remember Barry London and I heading up some monster hill in Marin one day in the early part of a long ride to Bolinas. As we approached the hill, he let out a big giant sigh and said, "Ahhh, a hill!" like it was some sort of wondrous thing, which it was. I got the message that hills are our friends, and if we approach each one of them with a good attitude we'll enjoy the climb, rather than endure it. Think about the longest hill you've ever climbed. The longest hill I've ever climbed took me an hour. Probably like you, I can do anything for an hour.

Once you have that attitude, hills become manageable pieces of time. You shift down and spin your way up them and before you know it, you are on the top. Where I seem to struggle is when I'm with a pack. I can either climb faster or just give up and go slowly, depending on what I've eaten that day, if my shorts feel too tight over my fat belly, or if I'm just not feeling my strongest. Then there's the pressure of the pack to get up the hill faster, which makes me feel stressed. Should you find yourself feeling this way, then go ride alone or with a slower friend. It's just not necessary to always go out and kill yourself with a pack of hard guys, sometimes it's great to have a mellow ride. In fact, I consider those the finest as you have time to enjoy the experience rather than suffer your way to the top, gasping for breath and trying to keep up.

Finding your rhythm

Ultimately, learning how to ride with the guys means learning how to first be comfortable riding with yourself. Finding your own comfort level then adjusting to their comfort level is key. Once you've mastered shifting, climbing, riding with a pack, and being an enduro mountain biker, you'll discover that hanging with other people who are faster better stronger than you isn't that bad once in a while. A steady diet of really stretching the envelope will feed your rat but can also be exhausting, so ride carefully. You need a few rest days now and then to allow your body to recover from all that adrenaline and sweat and breathing and lactic acid and heart rate stuff. You also should take slow rides with your friends who just want to chill out to keep yourself from getting so caught up with performance that you forget how much fun riding can be.
While you are out there, realize how wonderful it is that you have these great places to ride, and a body that is in shape enough to enjoy the ride. Think of those less fortunate in body than yourself, for they are legion. We are truly the lucky ones.

Sometimes love and cycling don't mix

Now it's time for me to really get on my soapbox. Here is: guys have a herd mentality. Not to say they aren't individuals, but get a group of regular guy friends together and you'll see that they are indeed different from us. And that's a good thing, but it places you into the category of "other." Think about it. Do you really want to date the guys you ride with or do you want to fit in with the crowd? You generally can't do both. There are always exceptions, of course, but in my experience if you want to ride with the guys it's best to keep everything on a friends only basis. Otherwise the guys will look at you differently when you show up to hang with the pack. It's not pretty, you will become an "outsider."

If you have dated even one of the guys in the pack, there will be the issue of ex boyfriends, or maybe if you've dated more than one of the guys then you are well, the meat on the hoof so to speak. You know what I mean, they act differently if you date them. I personally have found that going online to dating sites during my single years and meeting adventure friends who could turn into prospective boyfriends (more often than not they remained adventure friends) worked best. That way, everyone understands up front that you are both single, and both interested in meeting someone, but also just being adventure partners if it works out that way.

A lot of the adventure forum guys are already spoken for, so if you want to go online and find a boyfriend who's also an adventure pal, rather than look for him in the regular pack of guys you hang out with, you can use your computer savvy and writing talents to select and choose from the increasing number of available men out there on actual dating sites. Some are quite nice. I should know, I met my husband online after seven years of living alone on the mountain with my daughter and animals. I actually met him in person while working as the Bike Shop Service Manager for Eastern Mountain Sports in Albany, New York. That was good, because with recently shorn hair, a dirty black apron and grease under my fingernails, I was the epitome of my real self, and he liked me anyway.

When I met my husband, I had a lot of great male friends, but none of them were "boyfriends," because as I said before, dating the pack really muddies the waters and I like to keep things separate. I recommend you not confuse the two, because you may find that the man who you thought was of your dreams is really just a guy looking for someone to ride with, not a guy looking for a girlfriend.

If you are dating online, on the other hand, it's very useful to really know your stuff and what you are looking for in a mate, also to understand that yes, ladies, there are a lot of posers out there. You have to use a lot of savvy and don't spend too much time on email if you meet someone you like who fits the profile you are looking for, and above all, don't settle! Make a few calls, talk on the phone, then reevaluate whether you still like them. First second and third impressions are best. If you feel okay about it, go ahead and meet them for coffee or something. See if they seem angry, or seem to have problems that are not the kind of baggage you would want to carry around with you. I wrote a description of the perfect mate and wouldn't stop looking until I found him. Once I had my description written down, I knew that anything less wasn't the ultimate person I was looking for but that took me a few years to figure out. What I'm saying is, look for the one you really want, not the one who's available. Otherwise well, read on.

I met this one cyclist guy online and his online personae, talk and road biking photos were really brilliant, but after a few emails I realized he really had an anger problem so I pretty much wrote him off. Still, his photos and online profile really did look good and he kind of haunted me a little and I sort of wished in a way we could have talked more. One day I'm at the climbing gym, the really hardcore climbing gym where many of my friends hang out, and I see this guy who needs some help with a belay. I offer to belay him and coax him up the climb, then realize he was the guy I had emailed like, a year before. I could tell that in person he was just so totally not my type. Kind of like, yech. I'm sorry but he was truly yech. One of those guys who looks good on paper with titanium Serotta road bikes, and the whole deal.

In person, it was fun to help him up the gym wall but I was oh ever so grateful I didn't go beyond a few emails because when we met in person at one of my favorite haunts, there was no "aha, I remember you," to deal with. I walked out of there with my fantasy bubble burst, and without him in my life. It was a great lesson and a big relief.

On a good note, many of the male friends I met online through adventure sites, knowing we were looking for actual adventure partners, and not dates, are still my friends today, and they bring their new girlfriends around to meet me, some of whom are fantastic adventure women. So if you are going out there adventuring and looking for that perfect mate, or just someone to date, rather than eyeing the guys in your group, it's easier to go online to a dating site and chat with guys who are also single and looking. Otherwise you'll possibly find yourself in the uncomfortable and regrettable position of being the woman who someone's buddy dated and said, "She's fun for a while, but I don't really feel comfortable riding with her now." And neither will the rest of his friends, formerly your friends, now a reincarnated as a fast pack minus one.

Look at it this way, if you have a plan to find the right guy, write it down and stick with it. You'll end up with a guy who will adventure with you, be your mate, and also allow you to continue to keep all those great male pals who you have enjoyed as friends all these years on many an epic adventure.

And why shouldn't he?

After all, you've never dated them.

9

Bike repairs

"Marriage is a wonderful invention.Then again, so is a bicycle repair kit."

—Billy Connolly

This chapter is devoted to a discussion of simple and advanced bike repair. Before we get started, I'd recommend that you purchase real bike repair manuals if you are remotely interested in learning how to do most repairs yourself. My first bike repair book was *Glen's Bicycle Manual*, which I wore completely out. I progressed to working in bike shops as a fledgling mechanic, truing wheels with the help of Jobst Brandt's *The Bicycle Wheel*, then finally edited repair books for Rob van der Plas. Last year, my bike repair book library expanded to include Barnett Institute's four-book series. Being a fan of good tools, I will also share with you my favorite tools and describe how to set up your shop.

Please note: This chapter will only provide basic instructions to perform simple bike repairs as the aforementioned resources tell the advanced story so much better than I can. Get a good repair book that appeals to your mechanical senses. You'll be glad you did. You can follow my lead, get a job in a bike shop and really go crazy or just stick to the basics, it's up to you. Just in case you want to know how to expand your serious home repair shop, I'll include the best tools for the job. For example, if you want to learn to true wheels, you should invest in a Park wheel truing stand, just like they have in the bike shops. If you have multiple bikes, like I do, and service the family fleet, you should invest in a real bike repair stand, the type that weighs too much for you to carry around alone. If you prefer to install your own headsets, a headset press works much more efficiently than using just a block of wood and a hammer. I have

Craftsman wrenches, and a Pedro's race set (includes everything I need in a small package) which I take with me to the shop or on the road. These tools are not cheap, but they will allow you to fine tune your machines to perfection. I was fortunate to buy most of these major investments used from bike shops with friendly mechanics. The larger tools will never require replacement as they are built to last for many years. You'll probably wear out before they do.

We'll first discuss simple safety checks and bike repairs, then slightly more advanced bike repair, finally we'll review what to do at the shop to get your bike serviced.

Shall we begin? If you've read these chapters consecutively, you'll know what you need to do for a basic safety check. Just to be on the safe side (pun intended), I'll briefly reiterate that safety check here.

- Check wheels skewers for tightness
- Pump up the tires
- Spin wheels for trueness
- Check brake levers and brakes to ensure they work properly
- Check brake cables if brakes are loose
- Check handlebar stem for tightness
- Check headset adjustment to ensure it doesn't rattle or shake
- Check shifters and derailleurs to ensure they shift properly
- Check derailleur cables if shifting doesn't work properly
- Check crank for looseness
- Ensure drivetrain is clean and lubed
- Ensure that seat is level and adjusted to your body

Tools to carry on the road

- Alien multi-tool
- Pump

- Black, red or green spoke wrench
- Plastic tire irons
- Patch kit
- Duct tape
- Extra tubes

Additional tools for your home bike repair shop

- Park truing stand with multiple spoke wrenches (red, green and black)
- Park single repair stand
- Headset press
- Large adjustable wrench (for the older style headset)
- Craftsman or Sears metric wrench set
- Philips and flat smaller screwdrivers
- Pedro's crank tools, cassette remover, cone wrenches, headset wrenches
- Allen wrenches up to nine mm (for the crankset)
- A large work bench which I'll tell you how to make
- Pedro's chain lube
- Pedro's grease
- Rags, brushes
- Citrasolve

Note: bike cleaning and washing should occur outside, but never at the car wash! I'll say this again a few times just to remind you.

Setting up your shop

Let me describe my basement. I have the best basement in the world because it's my hangout place, my bike shop, my snowboard/ ski tune shop, and my skateboard shop. It doubles as the yoga room, the bike spinning room, and the skating room. I have an old TV, a radio and some candles. There are fluorescent lights everywhere, the dogs can visit through their dog door, and it's clean and dry. There's even a toilet and a sink! What more could a girl wish for in a shop? In the wintertime, at night and on rainy days this shop keeps me fully occupied and gives me a place to escape to when I need some alone time. Who says girls can't hang out in the garage/ basement?

If your husband or significant other has already staked out his own basement/garage space, work out a deal where you can also have your area and even do a time share. I will admit to being very possessive of my tools though, as bike tools are specific and replacing them can be a time consuming effort. I'd recommend you keep your space and your tools separate from his space and his tools. Kind of like some happily married couples are with their bank accounts.

My basement shop once was a dank, dingy but large area filled with stuff. I have slowly cleaned it out and reorganized it into a room of my own. It's not a "finished" basement per se so there's no fear of creating a mess on the concrete floor. I do have some exercise machine mats that I put down for the yoga classes and a great DVD collection (Sex in the City, award winning climbing videos, Freeboarding movies, and Shiva Rea's yoga classes) for when I'm down here working on stuff.

The first thing you want to do is build yourself a nice bench cheap. My husband made two sturdy four foot high sawhorses out of two by fours and clamps. Then, I purchased two 12 foot X 10 inch X 4 inch raw pine planks and placed them over the sawhorses for a very inexpensive and solid work bench. I also have two other work benches in the basement but this is my bench of choice as it's so tall and solid and smells so good?.

Now that you have your bench, you will want to place your bike repair stand near it, along with your tools which should be comfortably spread out in an open spot so you can find them. When working with small parts, always put down a towel or large rag to hold the smaller parts. Once they fall off the bike and roll under something you may never find them again. Imagine, losing one bearing from your wheel and not being able to ride your bike! That's happened to me and I used to only have one bike back in Oklahoma when I was a broke college student. Not being able to ride my one bike was truly heartbreaking, especially since it was also my transportation and my entire entertainment solution. Don't let it happen to you. While we are on the don't list, here's another biggie: specific parts fit in and on specific places on bikes. If you have the wrong size part or the wrong part, don't try to force it because it just won't work and you'll probably end up doing more damage than good if you keep trying to make it work.

Back in my Oklahoma days, I learned everything backwards, as in the wrong way. When my derailleur broke, I tried to take it apart and fix it. Wrong move. Never could get that little spring thing back in, so I tried using a spring from another junked derailleur. This took hours and never did work. Then there was the time that I took apart a freewheel, which they don't even make anymore but you can find them on older bikes. It didn't spin well so I thought to grease the bearings inside. Trouble is, those bearings are super tiny and not really meant to be taken out, replaced and lubed. In my efforts to get the thing working, I neglected to put down a towel, lost a few bearings on the floor and that freewheel was toast. Didn't get to ride that day. Remember, I had only one bike.

In another freewheel episode, I tried to replace a cog with broken teeth on the old freewheel with a new cog from the local bike shop, but I was missing the spacers and the new cog was not the correct size. To compound the issue, I had an old chain which had already "mated" with the older freewheel cogs, which meant the following happened:

The chain wouldn't correctly click shift to the cogs I installed because they were too far apart and too big for the derailleur. If I manually shifted the chain over to the new cogs, it skipped constantly as it had not mated with the newer cogs. Arrgghh!! After hours of work, I never did get to ride my bike that day. That freewheel was toast.

Then there was the time I stripped out my crank arm by trying to install a pedal on the wrong side of the bike. The crank is alloy, while the pedal axle is steel. Another time I stripped out the crank itself by allowing it to get too loose on the bottom bracket axle and not tightening it. Crank is alloy, bottom bracket axle is steel. That ruined crank was a very expensive mistake for a poor college student with one bike, no car, no TV, and no life without her bike. These are just a few of many examples I could share with you but rather than further embarrass myself and give everyone a good laugh, I'll provide some suggestions to avoid disaster during your first forays into bike repair.

Tips for successful repair

As with the English language, there are rules that govern correct usage with multiple exceptions. Remember the following bike repair tips and you'll have better luck with your tweaking:

Rightie tightie, leftie loosie is generally the case unless you are installing and removing pedals and other odd bits. In the case of pedals, they are marked left and right with an L and an R. The left pedal unscrews in a clockwise, or *rightie tightie* direction, while the right pedal unscrews in the traditional counter clockwise, or *leftie loosie* direction.

Excessive torque is something to be mostly avoided as the bike's sensitive parts are comprised of alloy connected to steel.

Lube everything with a little grease or bike lube, included brake cables and pedal spindles, but don't lube the bottom bracket cups. They require an adhesive agent such as blue Loctite.

A little goes a long way, especially when truing wheels. Always check for thread length before engaging in spinning action with your tools. Chances are something will strip if you are not careful and spin your tool too many times.

Check your tire(s) before installing a new tube. Find the cause of the flat before you try to remedy it, that way you won't end up with a brand new flat in the same spot.

Never wash your bike at the car wash. It may seem like a simple solution if you have a small apartment and no where to wash the massive amounts of mud off your bike, but you will discover that you have also blasted all the grease out of the bearings in the process, rendering your bike unridable. Yes, of course I did it once.

Always use correct tools that fit bike parts exactly, meaning always use metric. Standard tools do not fit metric bikes; all bikes and motorcycles are metric. Most home repair shops are comprised of standard tools because everything else, including automobiles, seem to be standard. Skateboards continue to confound me as they are sometimes metric, and sometimes standard (but that's a different book).

Don't put off tomorrow what you can adjust today. That slight rattle in the rear axle could be your cassette about to fall off during the ride.

At home, avoid catastrophes

First I'll discuss a few simple repairs you can make at home, then we'll go into a few simple repairs you can make on the road. Keep in mind what I just said above, don't put off tomorrow what you can fix in your shop today. It's much easier to nip a problem in the bud (as in the shop) than to replace a dangling cog that has fallen off the wheel because you didn't tighten that little screwring thing that holds it on. In fact, if you review my short list of field tools, I do not include cassette remover/tightener as one of them. You lose your cogset, you are walking your bike home. Same with not tightening your crank onto the bottom bracket. Same with not "loctiting" your bottom bracket cups. Etc.

The first thing you can do at home is again, I know this is repeat and boring, but do your basic safety check. Let's say you have a semi flat tire on the front of your bike and a hard tire on the back. Your seat is a little flexy cos you have a super light women's seat and it is hard to keep that puppy tuned up tight when you are gnarling with your crotch hanging on tight around curves. Hey, it happens. Your handlebar is slightly loose. Your headset rattles.

Get out your floor pump, and get those tires hard girlfriend! Do it now. For mountain bikes, I just make it hard for the uphill and take air out for the downhill. For road bikes, use the gauge on your floor pump to get the tires up to 120 psi for 700 X 23c or whatever the tire says it takes.

Your seat: Take the Allen wrench or open wrench that fits and tighten your seat to the seat post clamp. Again, yes, it came loose so just go do it. Use an Allen wrench to tighten your handlebars to the stem. Get out the headset wrenches and the really large adjustable wrench (usually 16mm) to adjust your older style headset, or some Allen wrenches to adjust the newer style headsets. For headsets, I'll suggest you purchase a bike repair book or have someone show you first, as there are bits and pieces within the headset/head tube that can come loose, your fork can fall off, and then you'll have a real problem.

Dirty bike

Deep in the heart of Northern California, you'll find a guy named Gravy. He's a wheel builder extraordinaire, in fact I have a set of bomber wheels with multicolor spoke nipples on my Breezer that he built me way back when we all hung out together. I think I have only trued them once or twice within the past 15 years of sometimes very hard and steady riding. Steve Gravenites, or Gravy as we all know him, has a bike shop in Marin County and always keeps a bike washing station nearby for those muddy mountain bikers who like to take decent care of their bikes and also refuse to stop riding just because Bobo got five inches of rain last night. I modeled my bike washing station after Gravy's, and here it is:

Set aside a spot in your yard that is equipped with a garden hose with a nozzle on it. Keep a long bristled brush handy, along with some cheap dishwashing liquid, some rags, and your favorite brand of lube. As mentioned, I'm a Pedro's fan but as long as it's bike lube, it's probably fine. Note: Tri-Flow, found in most hardware stores, is not a lube, it is a solvent. Solvents are for cleaning, not lubing, so if you spray your stuff down with Tri-Flow you are not doing your bike any favors. Anyway, back to the yard: I generally line up all the bikes that were ridden that day, and hose them down good. Then, flip them upside down, take the dishwashing liquid and squirt it on the dirtiest parts, namely the drivetrain and sometimes the bottom of the bike. Scrub with your brush, rinse, dry, lube.

Chain skips

What, your chain skips on your mountain bike? That's a piece of cake. Assuming you have a bike stand, place your bike on the stand and clamp it down tight on the seat post, not the seat tube. Isn't that satisfying? Take a moment to stare at your beauteous bike, the fabulous item that keeps your thighs toned and your belly flat. Oh and by the way, lesson learned, never ever clamp your bike on the seat tube, you'll wreck the frame. No, thank you, I've never committed this worst of all possible mistakes, but I've certainly considered it. While you are admiring your bike, slowly pedal it and watch the chain closely at the rear derailleur, what's the chain doing? When it skips, note that the link that skips is tight. Take both hands, grasp the link, and woman-handle tweak it from side to side. That's right, you are about to use brute strength on this otherwise delicate seeming piece of bike equipment.

Once you've worked your chain link from side to side, add some lube to it and continue to slowly pedal your bike, carefully watching the chain (like a hawk) and repeat the same business to each and every link that seems a bit tight. Lube that puppy up, wipe it off with a rag, and move on to the next item.

Chain falls off the crank on the inside

Oh, I get it, your chain is falling off on the inside of your bike when you shift into granny gear. Well, that's a common problem and the reason is your derailleur is over shifting, so first shift into granny gear and see how much slack you can take out of the cable. There's a clamp on the derailleur that holds the cable tight. Make sure you have a taut cable, if not, use your handy dandy Allen set and find the key that fits. No I'm not going to point it out to you, use a bike repair book if you can't figure this out. It's metric.

Your derailleur is hanging too far on the inside for a reason, and it's adjustable. Take a long hard look at the line up from the back wheel looking forward. Where's the derailleur facing, left or right? Left would be the inside, if you are really at the back wheel looking towards the front of the bike, and right would be towards the outside. I suspect it is facing left as your chain is falling off on the inside of the crank, as mentioned earlier.

If the derailleur seems to not be lined up exactly straight over the chain, you can loosen the clamp that holds the derailleur to the seat tube of the bike, and move the derailleur ever so slightly over to the correct direction, but first you have to loosen the cable that creates tension on the derailleur itself. Loosen the cable clamp on the derailleur, loosen the derailleur clamp, move the derailleur to line it up in a straight line over the chain, tighten the clamp bolt, then tighten the cable bolt. Should all work beautifully. If it doesn't you have to next check your derailleur screws.

First, look at your front derailleur screws. There is one with a minus sign and one with a plus sign. You'll see that one screw pushes the derailleur out onto the larger chainrings while one pushes the derailleur into the smaller chainrings. By closely examining your derailleur you can tell which end of the spectrum it is leaning towards, and using a small Phillips screwdriver, you can adjust the plus or minus screws accordingly. This is all just to make the chain not fall into the bottom bracket and trip you up big time during your hard drive downhill on some mountain road as you put the hammer to the pedal.

Chain falls off the crank on the outside

Review all of the above and adjust accordingly.

Chain skips a gear or falls off the rear derailleur

Wow, I can cram a bunch of information in here because the rear derailleur is less of a mystery than the front derailleur as long as you don't ever try to take one apart.

Check the chain for stiff links. You know what to do if you find one. Shift into the smallest chainring on the back and examine the rear derailleur cable. Is it loose? Adjust and tighten. Shift into the gear that skips and watch the chain run through the derailleurs from the rear wheel vantage point, is it skipping because the chain has a tight link, or because the derailleur isn't in a straight line? If it's not in a straight line, first slightly adjust the cable barrel on the rear derailleur. It's a finger adjustment. This should stop the problem.

If it doesn't, next look at your rear derailleur screws, the plus and minus signs. You can barely touch them and get the chain perfectly adjusted on the rear cogs but I'm warning you, touch them with caution. A little goes a long way with those plus or minus signs, I'd hate to see you in your bike shop basement screaming cuss words and swearing at the bike, all because you did what I said and it didn't work.

Look at the rear derailleur and chain from the vantage of the rear wheel facing forward, and you'll soon discover the zen of bicycle repair. You will see the slight moment where the chain is slightly crooked. Adjust that little nothing using all of the above techniques and you will be one happy bicyclist. Over do it and you have a serious puzzle on your hands. Get out your bike repair manual and go back to the beginning to reset your derailleur. I wish I was kidding. Here's another annoyance, how about your squeaking brakes?

Squeaking, squealing brakes

Tired of letting everyone know you are on the trail? Me too, so let's fix those brakes. First, take a look at them, which is how you will render an initial diagnosis for the majority of your bike problems. The brake pads *should* be what's known as "toed in," meaning the front of the pad should be touching the wheel before the rear of the pad. They should be flush to the rim of the brake, aligned evenly and of course, not touching the tire. Remember the flat discussion earlier? It could have been your brake pad, did you look at the tire before putting a new tube in? If the brake pad is unduly worn in any direction then you have to replace it. Here's a tip, if you took a long hard mud ride in the rain with lots of hills, you most likely will have to replace your brake pads. Don't worry, they aren't expensive. Here's how to reinstall/adjust your brake pads:

There's a little Allen bolt that holds the brake pad in place. First, loosen it, then place a match book top or a piece of thick paper between the rear of the brake pad and the wheel. Align the pad back up where it should be, tighten the bolt and you will have the required "toe in" space which will make your brakes stop squealing. Adjust both brake pads so that they are equally touching the wheel and you should be golden.

Flats

Here's the quick version: Flip your bike upside down, take the wheel off the bike, get your tires lever that's right, lever, not lever(s) out and stick it under the tire bead. Slide it carefully around the rim of the wheel and loosen the tire from the wheel. Take the tire off the wheel on one side only, feel with your fingers while doing a visual of the tire to make sure it wasn't a thorn or piece of glass that caused the flat. Next, check the rim of the wheel to ensure that the rim tape hasn't come off somewhere causing the flat by a spoke. Take a good look at your tube and try to find the spot that caused the flat, then recreate the scenario of your tube on the wheel with the tire to figure out where exactly the hole came from. I know this is detective work but if you do it now, your flat repair will stick, whereas if you don't do it now you'll just immediately or in the near future suffer another flat with perhaps no spare tube this time.

Hopefully you'll find the offending culprit in the tire, but if not and if the tire isn't blown as in has a hole in it, proceed on to getting your new tube out of your bike bag. Pump it up a tad, then place it within the tire. Reattach the bead to the wheel at the tube valve. Using your tire lever, slowly reattach the tire to the wheel by moving the lever slowly around the bead and using it to reattach the tire, rather than using your fingers or as some people I have known have done, a screwdriver. Check the tire for bulges. Pump up the tube a tiny bit. Check the tire for bulges again. If none are found, pump up your tire fully, reattach it to the bike, and pedal on, girlfriend. You have successfully repaired your first flat.

Broken chain

If your chain breaks and you don't have a chain breaker (i.e. the device found on your Alien multi-tool) you are walking home, or calling someone for a ride. There is no repairing a broken chain, even though I've seen many a person try with rocks, pliers, the guy at the gas station, you name it. If you have your chain breaker, line the tool up with the broken chain link and slowly noodle the little rod out of the link by slowly turning the handle of your tool, which attaches from one half of the Alien. An actual chain breaker minus the multi-tool is a single piece of equipment but works in exactly the same manner. The chain rod is a very small part that allows the chain link to link to other chain links. You will have to actually take a link out of the chain as it's probably ruined from breaking, and reattach the next link to the rest of the chain. Don't forget where the chain goes, through both derailleurs and onto the front and rear chainrings.

Remember this, once you remove the little rod from the chain link completely, it can't be replaced, so just noodle it on out to the edge of the link, slide the rest of the chain into that part, then noodle it back in. Your little chain breaker device has a great spot in it to set the chain, and with a few twists of the handle the tool does the rest. Remember, if you remove a link, your chain will be shorter, so please don't go into the larger chain rings until you've made it home and visited with your local bike shop for a new chain of the proper length if necessary. Repairing your chain on the fly is kind of like putting a spare tire on your car, you don't want to drive with it forever but you do need to get on down that road to where you are going.

Broken spoke

This is not good. If your spoke breaks and you haven't spent some serious time with Jobst Brandt's *Wheel Book* and with your wheel in a truing stand, don't try to fix it. You could regret ever twisting a spoke wrench one too many times. However, if you have a spoke wrench that fits your wheel's spokes (black, green or red), chances are, one of your riding friends or a passerby on a bike may be able to repair the wheel for you. If no one is available to help, then disengage the brakes from the wheel with the broken spoke to allow it to wobble freely, and slowly limp home with one brake. Get to the nearest bike shop and either have them replace the spoke, after which you can hop on your bike again and ride it, or purchase another spoke, go home, place your wheel on your Park truing stand and repair it yourself. This happens to everyone at least once, which is why I always carry a spoke wrench. By the way, I've done all of the above, including twisting a spoke wrench one too many times.

Well, now we can keep going or I can just say a few more words about bike repair and the mechanic mentality in general. If you really want to work on your bike, you can definitely find resources to do that and I applaud you for your ingenuity. Buy good tools! You are not overspending and you'll love your independence if you have your own shop. Start with one tool at a time, learn how to use it and progress to the next tool. It took me years to build my shop and I know how to use everything in it. Well, there was the time I broke the part on my ... maybe we won't mention that story here.

There aren't too many more new ways to fix old problems, but if you have some novel ideas, please send them to me as I'm always interested in hearing how problems can be solved in a new manner. These days, bike parts aren't really made to be repaired, which is a sad state of affairs to many of us. If your STI brake lever/shifter combo breaks you have to purchase a new set, rather than repair the separate brake/shifter mechanisms as you could back in the old days. I don't even want to talk about the advent of shocks and why I never wanted to have a bike with a shock and now I have three to maintain. Eek! Seems like everything is designed to throw away, and many of us wish for a return to the simple mechanicals that were made to last. However we are products of our times and admittedly, the new stuff just works better than the old stuff. More shocks equals less wrecks, certainly in my case anyway.

The bike shop mechanic

Yes, it's true, I still go to bike shop mechanics. They just know more than I do as they do this stuff all the time. When I have a problem with my shock, which I have had recently (no surprise!), I go to the Spoke in Williamstown to solve it. When I want to juice a few more miles out of my really worn out beater STI shifters that I bought used years ago, I go to my favorite mechanic Mike at

Plaines in Pittsfield who's been there for 32 years. He just knows sooo much more than I ever will. Once in a while, or all of the time, you may find yourself dealing with bike shop mechanics.

Here's what you do: First, clean your bike up. Take off all the mud, grime and grit, as much as possible. Hand the mechanic a clean bike, he/she will appreciate it. Diagnose your problem at home, at least down to the general area. For example, rather than, my bike needs a tune up, say, my bike doesn't shift right, the wheels wobble, the brakes are loose and my seat just hurts! They really appreciate it if you tell them what the problem is so they don't to spend all day trying to satisfy an unspoken request. If you really will need your bike at a certain time, first find out if they are booked solid that week, which they should never be by the way, and then be sure you don't need a really obscure part that they have to order, such as a specific new shock with X amount of travel. If you want that shock, fine, have them order it and bring your bike in after the shock is in their hot little hands. Time will fly and you'll be flying too, on your happy bike with a new shock. Another thing, and this should be unspoken, but bike shops generally are swamped on Saturdays.

That's like, the absolute worst day to take your bike in for a major repair if you want it back that day or the next. Check with them if you have to do Saturday. A spoke is one thing, a new shock is another. When you go to the shop, be nice to your mechanic. Find out who's working on your bike and take them a coffee, tea, sack of donuts, six pack of beer, a pizza, something to share with their fellow mechanics, whatever they like. They will appreciate it. And, it's not a bad idea to say thank you very much and even tip for a job well done. Hey, I've been tipped. I liked it! Stick with one or two shops and always go to your same people. They will remember you, remember your bike and remember which parts started to wear out and need repairs.

It's okay to ask their opinions on the rest of the bike if you have questions. Such as, do you think I should replace these brake pads? Or, I'd really like to get a new seat, this one has never felt right and now it hurts. Which would you recommend for someone of my size, riding ability, and bike style? Now I will tell you that if you ask for their opinions constantly and argue or never follow their advice, they will get tired of talking to you and you will become one of the dreaded Bad Customers. You don't want that title, believe me. Their time is valuable, their boss doesn't want them chatting all day long and they have a multitude of other customers who also want their bikes serviced ASAP.

Treat your bike mechanics with respect and they'll fine tune your bike and throw in the occasional extra touch of tender loving care. Someday they may even give you a good deal on that used Park truing stand they have sitting in their home bike repair shop or that practically new Park repair stand that they want to replace with a double stand but can't justify the expense unless you want to buy the single stand at a substantial (read wholesale) discount. Hey, it's happened to me. Besides, if they eat the donuts you won't have to.

10

Just bring the kids

"One of the most important days of my life was when I learned to ride a bicycle."

—Michael Palin

Pregnant!

I used to ride my old one speed bike in the basement. Once I was three months pregnant, I couldn't bend over the handlebars anymore. It was a big day when I discovered that my bike time was seriously curtailed. I was riding with Paul and the guys, hanging hard, trying to keep up and I went up and drafted behind Paul, trying to get his attention. I said Paul, my bro, I have a secret and please don't tell the guys I'm pregnant. He was pretty happy for me, being a proud father of two beautiful children, but I was still in shock at the idea that soon I would be forced off the bike. You see, for about 20 years, all I did was bike. I managed to get away with 35 years before having Reesa. Of course, she has enriched my life beyond comprehension, but at the time, it was just as hard for me to comprehend I was not alone anymore.

At about six months, even riding the bike in circles in the basement became too challenging for me. I was just so crushed, what in the heck was I to do now? A great friend who lives up the hill with her six children said to me, Jules, just quit whining and start hiking. And that's what I did, every day, even the day I went into labor with Reesa. She gave me some of the best advice ever, along with vacuuming while Reesa slept, putting her on the grown up potty, and using cloth diapers.

Reesa began her life in February of 1995, deep in the heart of New England's stormy winter. We hiked in two feet of snow when she was three days old. I put little hand warmers, the kind you use for skiing, inside her snowsuit. At 6.5 pounds, she was a perfect, tiny girl, and needed the extra heat for her arms and legs. She slept through our hike, nestled deep inside my front baby pack. We started Reesa with gear. Her first was the front pack from the Mountain Goat in Williamstown. I also began hiking with her inside her sling, once she was a little older. At six months, she rode in my Kelty backpack. At one year, it was time for her to go for a ride in the baby jogger. Wow, what an awesome vehicle. It totally took the weight off of me, and with the addition of 24 inch mountain bike tires, we were ready to go off up through the hills on some really long hikes.

I almost felt like I was back on the bike, but not quite. True, I was riding again with the guys from the Spoke when Reesa's father would allow me to escape. By this time, I enjoyed taking her with me so much that I was anxious to have her with me, somehow, on the bike. I wanted to share my experience of rolling along with the wind in my hair and bugs in my eyes well, maybe not the bugs in my eyes part, with Reesa. Even at the early age of one, she was my primary adventure partner and I loved having her along for the ride, even on mommy's back and in the jogger.

The kid and the bike

It was finally time to put Reesa in the bike trailer. Back then they were uber expensive in bike shops. Since I couldn't afford the real version, I bought something heavy and sturdy from a big box store, and strapped her in tight. Let me describe this monster to you. It was a big wide plastic container with a chest strap and roll bars. It weighed a ton but was bombproof and affordable. These days, almost anyone can afford a decent trailer from your local bike shop. Think of it this way, how much is your kid worth?

Now, I'll go out on a limb here with my very unpopular and politically incorrect opinion about bike seats for the baby. I personally don't like them. Sure, you can get one for $75 bucks rather than$150, and it takes up less space than a bike trailer if you have a small living space. Those two things are the primary selling points for bike seats. Those are the ONLY good things about a bike seat for your child. Let's look at the pros and cons of trailers versus bike seats, but first I want to describe to you the mechanism of injury should you wreck your bike and fall over on your side. In a word, think blunt trauma to the baby's head and body. Think that helmet will protect your child from the massive force that occurs when a bike falls over with the baby's head bounces off the pavement? What's to protect your child if you happen to wobble and then fall down? Who's to say you can guarantee that you are such a great rider that you won't someday have a wreck, especially with an extra 20 to 75 pounds of kid on the back rack?

Sorry to be so graphic but a lot of people just don't realize what can happen in the event of the unexpected. Since I spend so much time analyzing rock climbing and white water kayaking accidents, I always envision the total possibilities to be as safe as possible. As opposed to the baby bike seat, the bike trailer has built in safeguards in case of rider problems. It also has many other great points about it, which I will now describe. First and foremost, the bike trailer has a roll bar to protect baby should you flip your bike. The trailer also has a pivot which will allow it to remain stable even if you do flip your bike. The trailer is equipped with full on chest straps, a rain fly, a bug net, and spots where you can stash water bottles and food for your child. The trailer has a flag, but I'd suggest you only ride with baby on unpopulated roads. Don't trust your baby's life to other drivers. In my experience, they have absolutely no mercy.

The bike trailer

The trailer folds up and can be stashed and transported quite easily. It is light and well-designed to ensure your baby's comfort and safety and unlike a baby bike seat, you can use it until they are around four years old. Even if you get caught outside in a sleet storm, your baby will be comfy, warm and dry inside her trailer. The very first day I took Reesa out for a ride in her trailer, she was singing the whole way. We rode up mountains and even came home to ride up my driveway. Anyone who's seen my driveway knows, most people don't even want to drive up it. I found such pleasure and joy in taking my daughter for her first ride and many rides afterwards. I was finally really back on my bike, and I had my little buddy with me the whole way. Wow!

Next comes those years when your child is too big for the trailer, and not big enough for a real bike yet. What I did was get Reesa a trike and let her ride it in the house. That was her experience with "training wheels." She took a while before she became comfortable on two wheels, as we went straight from the trike to a really sweet Diamondback BMX bike that both of us still ride.

Reesa never had training wheels. I think training wheels are great for some kids, as they help them balance, and certainly they work well with the smaller children's bikes. Once you get into BMX bikes, you have to just go for it. After a few wrecks, Reesa was cruising along at a good clip. One day during a ride down Mattison Hollow from our house, she surprised me and said Mom, I can ride your mountain bike. She was referring to my 16.5 inch Breezer, which I was riding at that time. I was like, no way dude, you can't ride my mountain bike, you are only 11! She convinced me to let her try, I lowered the seat and off we rode. She had the necessary clearance and handled the bike like a champ. When your child grows up suddenly, you may find yourself shocked, so prepare to get her a new bike.

The between years

As an aside, during the trike to BMX years, Reesa and I spent a lot of time climbing as that was a sport she could do with me most of the time. If I wanted to ride hard I occasionally went without her but I really enjoy her company so instead of riding alone, I hooked Reesa up with my kid-friendly climbing friends in the Gunks (Paul and Vitek, you know who you are) and we took her climbing all over the place. When she was really young, around five, I used to put a helmet on her, harness her up with her chest harness, anchor her in behind a tree, hand her some snacks and water, and keep her safe that way. We could climb on hard stuff and Reesa would rope up just for the approach, then happily hang out while mommy fell repeatedly on the 5.11 face problem.

My friends are so cool, they would pack extra snacks just for the ravenous little girl who would someday grow up to ride my mountain bike. Paul had a wide assortment of kids climbing shoes as he had three sons, there were lots of other kids in the Gunks, thanks to Jannette (cliffmama.com), and Reesa soon became known as a Gunks kid, meaning she could cruise the neighborhood with her wandering band, hanging out and making acorn stews when she wasn't climbing. Reesa has always been fearless, so by the age of six she was climbing three pitch climbs in the Gunks. She still to this day has an agile ability to climb harder stuff. Since I never forced her to climb, she also still enjoys the sport.

At the Charlemont kayak festival in 2004, Reesa decided she wanted to be in the climbing competition. While other kids, most notably a 14 year old boy were practicing all day long, up and down the EMS climbing wall, Reesa and her girlfriends spent their time happily eating chocolate, getting vendors to give them swag, and drinking copious amounts of free Red Bull. Drinking Red Bull? Reesa, put that down! My friends tell me they still remember when she took the wall, waltzing up it like it was nothing. True, the 14 year old boy who practiced all day won the competition, but only by a few seconds. Reesa was nine years old.

Do I sound like a proud parent? I am, and you should proud of your kids too. Children love having their parents impressed with them, and that means being happy if they come in second and even if they don't want to go adventure that day, and just want to talk to their friends online or go to the mall. As the title of this chapter says, ladies, just bring the kids. If your adventure friends aren't kid friendly, then get new friends. If you are interested in becoming a climber, go to www.rockclimbing.com and find someone in your area if there's no local climbing gym or store. Right now, I've got to go rescue my mountain bike from Reesa, she's heading out the door with it. Reesa, bring my bike back!

11

Living green

"If I can bicycle, I bicycle."

—David Attenborough

It's really time for us to join together and take back the streets, the forests, the paths and alleyways of the biking life. How does one go about creating a new, more humane world? We can start by being nice to each other.

Daily affirmations

Goal setting really works. In that same notebook where you keep your food diary, you can also write down your goals. First, figure out what those goals are. Do you want to eat better, sleep better, be better at your sports, a nicer person, a happier being? Are you looking for a new, lasting love, a different job, some best friends? Then write these things down and believe your dreams will come true.

Next, put your money where your mouth is. If you don't like certain corporations, don't shop there. Period. If you really feel bad about the elderly woman across the hall in apartment 2B who is all alone every day with no one to talk to, take her some cookies and start knocking on her door. If you are concerned about animal rights, become more vegetarian and seek out farmers or food distributors that support organizations who only practice humane animal treatment. Buy non-animal tested cosmetic and body care products. Eat less meat! Become a vegetarian! What's stopping you? If you feel concerned about your health due to what you've been told by others, then get out there and do your research.

Now find a way to volunteer your time somewhere. It could be as simple as visiting the elderly lady down the hall, volunteering for the local Humane Society, or you could even join the Peace Corps.

What's stopping you? If your friend is in need help that person out when they are in need, not when it's convenient for you.

Bike path activism

Miriam and her girlfriends are still chillin' on their favorite bike path. One day as they were enjoying their traditional four mile ride with a wine and dine, they started talking about other people in the world who were less fortunate than themselves. The three women quickly realized that right in their own area people didn't have what they had. Their conversation went something like this:

"I wonder how some of the poorer migrant workers around here manage to get decent food," Miriam asked her friends as they enjoyed a fresh sourdough loaf from the local organic bakery spread with soft sheep's milk cheese from the local organic farm. "They work picking veggies and fruit for these fancy restaurants, but I doubt they get to eat what they pick," she said.

"They sure do look hungry, especially the kids," Mary agreed. "Maybe there's something we could do to spread awareness. Does anyone know anyone who might help us get closer to these people? I don't speak Spanish." She looked ruefully at her half eaten sandwich. Suddenly it was much less appealing.

Sarah put her sandwich down, and took a sip of wine. "Well, my friend knows someone who has a housecleaner who's Mexican. Her name is Maria and she speaks a little English although my friend doesn't talk to her much about her life. Maybe Maria might know someone from the farms."

Miriam nodded. "There's a migrant trailer park over behind the new mall, seems like that might be a place where we could do something to help out." The three women sat silently, no longer savoring their food. Each of them struggled with the idea of how to do something to help these people who had so little yet gave so much. They all thought the migrant worker encampment might be a good place to start if they were looking for hungry people.

All of a sudden, Mary's face brightened and she began excitedly to talk. "I know exactly what we can do and we don't need anyone to help us!" she exclaimed. "We can ride our bikes to the trailer park and take everyone a big picnic lunch!" The girls all agreed, thrilled to finally be doing something about a problem that had been bothering each of them for quite some time, as there were many very poor migrant workers in their town, and they all looked sad, forlorn, and hungry. Not worried about the possible "dangers" of spending time in a migrant worker camp, they quickly mobilized and created a shopping list that day. The next day they met, hooked up Mary's child trailer to Miriam's bike (she was the strongest rider), and filled it with fresh foods for a wonderful feast at the little camp behind the Mall. Instead of their usual four mile wine and dine, they set off that day with another mission in mind, and rode almost five miles to the camp.

Several hours later at around six p.m., the tired girls finally arrived and parked their bikes in the middle of the encampment, where they spread out the big checkered table cloth that Miriam had previously used for her dining room table. Soon, the migrant workers and their children wandered over to see what was happening. Mary, Miriam and Sarah piled fresh loaves, washed fruits, aged gourmet cheeses, and bottles of organic juice for the children and a few select bottles of wine for the adults onto the checkered tablecloth. Paper cups, napkins, knives and forks were carefully placed within reach at the edges of the table cloth. Miriam began pouring juices and slicing the cheese. She beckoned to a hungry child and held out a handful of fresh strawberries with a nice chunk of cheddar cheese and a baguette. He shyly stepped forward and accepted her offering, breaking his fast for that day.

Even though the workers didn't speak English and the girls didn't speak Spanish, their intent to share their lunch was recognized by all and soon they had a happy and boisterous party going on with merry making, happy eating and even a few tears in the eyes of the older migrant workers who truly had never experienced the kindness of strangers in this land of plenty called America.

Thus began the humble non-profit organization "Feasts for Workers," which has spread throughout the Berkshires and has chapters in ten counties. Miriam, Sarah and Mary can still be found twice weekly enjoying their traditional wine and dine, but now they have included 50 to 100 migrant workers in their festivities, and use Mary's van to haul their feast to the masses. By the way, they still ride their bikes on the bike path every week, and due to the work involved in getting the big migrant worker food offerings together every week, all three of them have lost over twenty pounds each, much to the consternation of their husbands.

Trips for kids

Betty was always such an outdoorsy type A personality, she understood how it felt to be cooped up inside an airless building, feeling trapped and unable to move. She knows how depression works, and often remembers how she suffered growing up, never fitting in and always fighting the establishment. That attitude served her well as an adult because she never gave up on anything once she set her mind to it, which enabled her to complete law school and work in a top firm. Now as a national mountain bike racing champion, she could sort of relax in a way, because she no longer felt trapped and was so much happier with her life. She began to look around and notice the scores of kids who didn't seem to have anything to do with their time. They also didn't seem to have bikes.

Betty went online and googled kids on bikes, discovering that Trips for Kids had a chapter in her town. She emailed the address provided and offered to get involved in some way with the group. Always looking for volunteers, the director quickly contacted Betty and invited her to join her group on a ride up the local mountain pass that following weekend. Betty took a day off from training and joined the rag tag group, noticing how beat up their bikes were and what sad shape they were in. She immediately saw her opportunity and suggested that she tune up some bikes for them. That initial bike tune up led to Betty teaching the kids to work on bikes, which led to Betty apprenticing a couple of the kids and getting them jobs in local bike shops. Meanwhile, Betty had a chance to hang out with some truly disturbed kids and talk with them about their lives. A typical conversation went like this:

"My bike sucks!" exclaimed 12 year old Molly with unruly blond hair, torn and faded jeans, nose and lip piercing. It's the wrong color and I hate it!" She threw the offending pink bike down onto the pavement and stalked off. Betty had never seen the child's mother, only an older man who dropped her off on Saturdays and quickly sped away. She picked up the offending bike and rested it against the Trips for Kids van. Molly was sulking in the grass, sitting all alone. She seemed to expect Betty to do or say something but Betty had already seen this type of behavior many times, and used to act that way herself as a child. She ignored Molly and continued tweaking the third of ten bikes that were to be ridden that day. Molly's bike remained untouched. She began to get a concerned look on her face. "What's the deal, aren't you going to fix my bike?" she asked.

"Nah, it sucks," said Betty. "You really shouldn't ride it if it's the wrong color."

"But how will I go with you guys?" asked Molly, reality creeping in as she realizes that she's going to be left behind. "I don't have a bike to ride!" Tears began to well up in her sad blue eyes.

"Well, I dunno, I guess you won't go with us then," answered Betty, still not looking at her. She gazed up at the beautiful mountain trail they were to ride that day, then over at the boisterous group of children happily milling about, trying on helmets and filling their water bottles.

"I don't want to stay here by myself," cried Molly, tears streaming down her face. "I'm alone all the time at home too and I hate it!" She ran over to the bike, picked it up, and carefully rubbed at a scratch made when she threw it down on the street.

"I guess maybe you could come with us," Betty answered, finally looking at Molly. "But you'll have to tweak the bike yourself as I'm pretty busy here with all these," gesturing to the seven bikes still waiting to be adjusted, pumped up and lubed.

"I could do that," said Molly, already checking her tires for pressure. "Maybe I could help you with the other bikes too. I know how to pump them up, can I do that?" A streak of dirt ran across her face where the tears and dried into splotches of brown.

Betty stopped what she was doing and handed Molly the bike pump. "Yeah, that works," she agreed. Betty appeared deep in thought for a moment, as if pondering something serious.

"Hmmm, I've got an idea, if you can pump the tires really good, maybe you can help me out with all these bikes once in a while. Molly excitedly nodded and began to aggressively pump up her bike. She was smiling now, and had a mission.

Betty looked for a long moment at Molly. "I used to be alone when I was a kid too, and it sure isn't much fun. Want to tell me about it?"

Molly sniffled a little, removed the pump head from her front wheel, attached it to the rear tube valve and began to fill the rear tire of her bike. She kind of shook her head for a moment as if to clear the cobwebs. Betty waited patiently for Molly to talk, because once she began to talk, all the hurt that was inside of her could come out and she could begin to heal in the company of her newfound friends, the faithful mountain bike steeds and their riders.

"I guess it all started when my mom died," she said in a whisper. "My stepdad doesn't like me and sometimes he's mean to me." She looked up to see if there was shock on Betty's face, which only reflected compassion and concern. "I am thinking of running away," she added, "maybe to San Francisco."

"I can understand that," Betty said, displaying no surprise on her face. "How about if you just hang out with us riding bikes for a while instead? This is a fun group and I really need your help fixing these bikes. I can teach you to true wheels too so you can get a good job in a bike shop I know about when you are 15."

Molly's face brightened for the first time in a long time. "You mean you'd let me work with you and I could learn to do what you do?" she asked. "Wow, that would be so cool! You know what I'd really like to do?" She leaned in closely so that only Molly could hear as she whispered her secret. "I'd really like to race mountain bikes and be a national champion racer like you someday."

Betty held back a few tears of her own as the emotional floodgates opened and healing began in yet another misplaced child. "I can teach you that too," she said softly.

The original inspiration for Trips For Kids came in 1986, when founder and director Marilyn Price was pedaling up Mount Tamalpais, gazing at the view of San Francisco. She remembered the kids she used to see when she volunteered at St. Anthony's Dining Room in the heart of the inner city and thought how wonderful it would be if these kids, who she knew had never had the chance to do what she was doing, could join her. Many of those kids had never seen their city from that perspective. Most had never challenged themselves physically. And all spent their days surrounded by cement as well as constant exposure to drugs, violence and gang involvement. It was then that Marilyn's vision of Trips For Kids began to take shape. (from the website)

Animal dreams

Jules lives out in the country with her family. She's got some outdoor animals which is a good thing because they are required to build soil for gardens. These upstate NY hills are rocky and not much can be planted where Jules lives without some extra help from Mother Nature's pet goats and llamas. Jules' family heats with a woodstove, using a minimal amount of oil in their energy efficient oil furnace. She drives a four wheel drive vehicle with over 190k miles on it, and spends a lot of time outdoors with her children, animals, gardens, and friends. She loves her pets, many of them are rescues. They provide a lot of local entertainment when she and her daughter are not busy hiking the woods, looking for fairy houses. A typical day might be like this:

Well, today we'll have to go do something. My llamas would like some company not that they'll let me pet them of course. Babette is the wild one, she's curious but standoffish. Arpeggio plays the part of the overgrown bully teenager, Andante is my sweet beautiful girl who loves me, and Coconut is a pretty little white fella who regularly beats everyone else up, even tho he's small and scrawny. He just doesn't know it. I could go hang out in their barn with them and let them sniff me. Babbie and Coco are rescues from Northeast Llama Rescue. I'm glad to have them. I feel like we have an animal sanctuary here, although at times it does get pretty loud.

Later we'll head on up the pass at Misery Mountain. The Taconics lie next to the Berkshires and are equally as beautiful. There's a great hike up some creek beds that leads to the crotch of the mountain where we can look out from way high up and see everything, but everything can't see us. I like to hide out once in a while. My husband and I are debating the merits of taking our latest Weimaraner rescue Bella up the mountain with us. She's a wild one who used to be in a house with a sweet little old lady who had no fenced yard. Of course Bella waged maximum destruction on anything within her path that was chewable. My husband wants to know if we should feed the really old salsa in the fridge to Bella, or throw it out on the compost pile. The fact that she'll eat really old salsa tells you a lot about Bella.

There's eleven animals here, not counting the humans. I have been finding mice heads and limp mice bodies on the stoop outside the cat door. The cats are afraid to bring them into the house anymore because I throw them outside and then Bella eats them. We sighted some pheasant, grouse and bunnies down the driveway, which is amazing as the cats have decimated everything smaller than themselves for a quarter mile radius around our place. Gnarly little sisters, they are true Berlin, NY girls.

The goats have remained in their yard today so I don't have to do any fence repair although I should probably rebuild the whole thing. Too lazy I guess. They'll break out right when the sunflowers get tall and eat them. Happens every year. This year I beat them to the punch and erected a temporary llama fence outside the house so the llamas could have first dibs on the sunflowers and Jerusalem artichokes. I'm glad someone got something to eat that day.

I used to take my llamas for walks back before Arpeggio decided he was too big to be haltered. At 300 pounds he may be right, but I still need to get a handle on him. Once I sent him off to be retrained, and when I went to get him in my friend's minivan, he lay down sheepishly with his head on my lap, very glad to be back in my care. Yet once we got home he forgot about that sweet moment and started bossing me around again. Jeeze! Men! So it's off the llama yard I go. We'll clean the woodstove, start a new fire for the boys, then head up the mountain to play in the woods for a while. I hope all your animals get something good to eat today.

What to do

Jules used to be an EMT/firefighter and some would say that histrionic rescue mentality never left even though she's no longer on a local squad. Now, she rides for the National Ski Patrol in the winter, and rescues animals year round. Her work with Northeast Llama Rescue includes taking in two unwanted and often unruly beasts, helping the founder with non-profit applications, and website consultation. She is involved in all-breed rescue, and has assisted in rescue transfers, also taking in a Weimaraner pup who was too much for her previous owner. That makes two rescued dogs, and recently, a new Rottweiler puppy who started out life happy and is the sweetest, most loveable dog. Zuchini is a great example of how dogs can be when they are treated well from day one.

Someday, Jules hopes to contribute even more time and effort into rescue work. For now, she contents herself with the feeding, caring and loving of any animal who wanders onto her beaten path.

She is very interested in helping younger people overcome hurdles that life throws them, so she takes her daughter's friends to Kripalu yoga classes, rock climbing, kayaking, skiing, snowboarding, skateboarding and biking. She believes that keeping kids busy with fun outdoor activities and with inner growth experiences will help them deal with whatever problems they may encounter as growing teens.

A few last words

Shouldn't we do more to help our world? Think about it. It's simple to pierce the veil, but first we must pierce it with our hearts.

What can you do today to make someone's life easier? That someone can be a dog, a cat, a llama, a person. Rescue is real. Try it to ease your depression. I'll provide links on a resource page, but for now, just give it some thought. For example, if you have room, you can rescue a llama and its llama friend. Or if you have a truck, you can help your friend move. With tools you can fix someone's bike. With nothing you can be nice to an old lady. If you have something, maybe you can even take your llamas to visit nursing homes on Sundays in your minivan. You get the idea.

What if each one of us were to stop shopping at places we don't like? Think about it. Could we pierce the veil and gain enlightenment? What if you and I and everyone else lived in community and got along? We could share gardens! We could learn to speak without talking. We could hear our friends voices in our ears before they called us on the phone. The veil is so thin, it's falling away with every sweet word we speak.

We are happy and we live in peace.

Say it sister.

12

Resources

"Nothing compares to the simple pleasure of a bike ride."

—John F. Kennedy

This is the end. Before signing off, I want to leave you with some ideas so that you can create your own bike stories. In this chapter you will find a brief sketch of resources to get you started. The best way to find your own personal online place is to just start searching. If you are looking for bike people in Mississippi, for example, just go to your favorite search engine and type in "bikes Mississippi," or "bike clubs Mississippi," and you'll eventually find someone like minded to ride with or hike with or just talk to about biking. Also you can go to forums and blog blog blog. There are so many cool people out there, just waiting for your blog to appear. Type photonicgirl into a search engine and you'll find my big mouth blogging all over the universe on a wide variety of things. You can create your own free blog at: *www.blogspot.com*, which I have also done (see Adventures in Living below).

If you need assistance finding that special blogspot, I'm available and will happily respond to your questions, especially if you are somewhere in "Not obviously bike friendly Coldtown, South Dakota," for example. I promise you, there's a bike club even there, waiting for you. They may be really a snowshoe club, which is fine, because cross training is what it's all about. We grow as human beings by branching out, getting out of our small comfy space and becoming galactic humans who know and do all kinds of wonderful things. Stretch your brain, let yourself go, find a group and make some new friends. Use this chapter as a resource to open your mind with ideas of how to find your own niche club, group, coffee klatch, bike group. Our friends are here, we just need to reach out and touch them.

Local northeast groups

Adirondack Mountain Club (www.adk.org)

ADK is a 30,000-member nonprofit organization dedicated to the protection and responsible recreational use of the New York State Forest Preserve, parks, wild lands, and waters. ADK employs a balanced approach to outdoor recreation, advocacy, environmental education, and natural resource conservation. There are 27 local chapters throughout New York and in New Jersey and Massachusetts. Founded in 1922, ADK conducts extensive trails, education, conservation, and natural history programs.

Adirondack Sports and Fitness (www.adksports.com)

Adirondack Sports & Fitness is a unique monthly magazine—print and online—covering the Capital-Saratoga Region, Adirondacks and surrounding areas of New York State. Since 2000, it has been the essential guide for outdoor sports, recreation and fitness enthusiasts who live or play in the region.

Adventures in Living (www.photonicgirl.blogspot.com)

This site covers everything about life in the wild zone including dogs, cats, bears (bears?), snowboarding, white water paddling, rock climbing, llama rescue, living with farm animals, building gardens with cattle panels and anything else I can think of writing about. If you like alternative stuff and are into permaculture, organic food and playing outside, this is a blog you'll enjoy.

Appalachian Mountain Club (www.outdoors.org)

The Berkshire Chapter of the Appalachian Mountain Club, representing Western Massachusetts.

Berkshire Cycling Association (www.berkshirecycling.org)

Berkshire Cycling Association (BCA) is a bicycle racing club in the Berkshire Hills of Western Massachusetts.

Berkshire Sports (www.berkshiresports.org)

A website that details adventure events in the Berkshires

Camp Becket (www.bccymca.org)

Camp Becket YMCA...the yearning just to relax and talk openly with other boys the opportunity to try and even fail, without censure the freedom to explore the arts the willingness of young adults to communicate and to listen the rusticity of the cabin and the automat contrasted with one's home the erasing of artificial barriers such as religion, race, social standing the sweetness of clear air and clean water.

Farm and Wilderness (www.farmandwilderness.org)

Guided by the Quaker belief that the Light of the Spirit is present in every person and the belief that people working together can create a more just and humane society, the Farm & Wilderness Foundation sponsors year-round experiences for children and adults that emphasize the building of community through the values of cooperation, simplicity, responsibility, empathy, spirituality, and service. We are a 501(c)3 non-profit foundation.

Green Mountain Bicycle Club (www.thegmbc.com)

The Green Mountain Bicycle Club, formed in 1968, is the largest cycling club in Vermont, consisting of over 200 individual and family members. These enthusiasts represent a wide variety of cycling interests, among them general fitness riding, recreational riding, mountain biking, and competitive racing. The club has become involved in several programs open to the public, such as a practice criterium series, time trials, group rides, weekend tours, a winter lecture series, children's bike rodeos, and one of New England's most popular races, the Burlington Criterium.

Holiday Farm (www.holidayfarm.com)

A Community, a Family and a Farm Protecting the rural Berkshire landscape and sharing the benefits.

Mohawk Hudson Cycling Club (www.webmhcc.org)

The Mohawk Hudson Cycling Club consists of over 700 members who live and cycle in the greater Capital District area of eastern New York State. MHCC sponsors road and also mountain bike rides within an 80-mile radius of the Albany-Schenectady-Troy area, led by MHCC members for beginning through experienced riders. Curious? Just attend any MHCC event and experience the camaraderie and excitement for yourself.

New England Mountain Bike Association

(www.nemba.org)

NEMBA is a recreational trails advocacy organization. Our mission, which we've chosen to take, is to ride on the best trails that the world has to offer. Luckily, most all of them are in New England, so we don't have to travel far. We dedicate ourselves to taking care of the places that we ride, preserving open space, and educating the mountain bike community about the importance of responsible riding.

North Atlantic Velo (www.northatlanticvelo.org)

Welcome to the home of North Atlantic Velo. Founded in 2003 to promote racing in the Northeast and bring riders together for Road, Offroad, and Cyclo-Cross events. We are a regional team with riders in New York, Vermont, Connecticut, Massachusetts and New Hampshire. What we all have in common is that we race (a lot). NAV riders competed in over 400 Days of racing in our region and beyond in 2005.

Out of Control Ski Club (www.ocskiclub.org)

The O.C. Ski Club is one of the largest and most active ski clubs in the Northeast. It was established in December of 1960 as a Not for Profit organization. The Club's main objective is to promote skiing within the membership by running organized day, weekend, and week-long ski trips at economical prices.

The Narragansett Bay Wheelmen (www.nbwclub.org)

The Narragansett Bay Wheelmen is a bicycle club serving Rhode Island, Eastern Connecticut and Southeastern Massachusetts

The Saratoga Social Club (www.saratogasportandsocial.org)

The Saratoga Sport & Social Club is a *member driven organization* whose mission is to promote a sense of community between outdoor enthusiasts, clubs and businesses. Since its inception in the winter of 2005, over 500 members have expanded their circle of friends, found adventure hiking, skiing, biking, kayaking and climbing among other pursuits, and developed important networking opportunities along the way. The Club also plays a role in promoting an appreciation for the wild spaces we share in Saratoga County and the Adirondack Park region. We are always looking for ways to protect and preserve natural habitat... all while having a great time in the process!

Local and National Advocacy

Berkshire Bike Path Council (www.berkshirebikepath.com)

Facilitating bike path development in Berkshire County Massachusetts since 1998

Bikes Belong (www.bikesbelong.org)

Bikes Belong Coalition is a membership organization founded by bicycle industry and advocacy leaders with the mission of "putting more people on bikes more often."

Bike New York (www.bikenewyork.org)

Bike New York is a non-profit organization established in 2000 to promote and encourage bicycling and bicycle safety education through education, public events and collaboration with community and government organizations. Bike New York produces the largest cycling tour in America, the Five Boro Bike Tour.

League of American Bicyclists (www.bikeleague.org)

The League of American Bicyclists (America's oldest cycling organization) began when bikes, not cars, ruled the roads. Today, this organization is a leader in advocating and educating on behalf of cyclists in every state. They also organize major cycling rallies and support many local and state cycling groups across America.

Massachusetts Bicycling Coalition (www.massbike.org)

The primary purposes of MassBike are: to serve and protect the interests of the bicycling public in Massachusetts, to promote the bicycle as a healthy, enjoyable, efficient, and environment-friendly means of transportation and recreation, to promote a physical geographic context and vehicular traffic environment that enhance these qualities and ensure the safety of transportation by bicycle, and to help more people adopt the bicycle for transportation and recreation. The primary means by which MassBike achieves these goals are: advocacy on behalf of bicyclists before public bodies, including elected officials and government agencies, dissemination of information to the public and private industries, education of bicyclists and motorists concerning safe riding skills, good driving habits, and the rules of the road, and sponsorship of public events, both independently and in cooperation with other organizations.

New York Bicycling Coalition (www.nybc.net)

Welcome to the New York Bicycling Coalition! Increasing Education Safety and Access for all bicyclists in New York is our Mission.

International Mountain Bicycling Association (www.imba.com)

The mission of I.M.B.A., the International Mountain Bicycling Association, is to promote mountain bicycling opportunities which are environmentally and socially responsible.

Pedals for Progress (www.p4p.org)

Pedals for Progress rescues bicycles destined for America's landfills and puts them to work overseas for continuing economic development in our partnership programs.

Rails-to-Trails Conservancy (www.railstotrails.org)

RTC is a nonprofit organization working to enrich America's communities by creating a nationwide network of public trails from former rail lines and connecting corridors.

Surface Transportation Policy Project (www.transact.org)

The goal of The Surface Transportation Policy Project is to ensure that transportation policy and investments help conserve energy, protect environmental and aesthetic quality, strengthen the economy, promote social equity, and make communities more livable.

Trips for Kids (www.tripsforkids.org)

Trips for Kids (TFK) is a non-profit that provides mountain bike outings and environmental education for kids who would not otherwise be exposed to such activities. At our outings, we teach lessons in personal responsibility, achievement and environmental awareness through the simple act of having fun.

STRIDE (www.stride.org)

STRIDE, Inc. is a non-profit, volunteer organization dedicated to providing year-round recreational and leisure programs to individuals with special needs in a safe, fun, and educational environment.

USA Cycling (www.usacycling.org)

USA Cycling is the official cycling organization recognized by the US Olympic Committee and is responsible for identifying, training and selecting cyclists to represent the United States in international competitions. The major activities of USA Cycling ensure the ongoing development and safe participation in the sport of cycling.

Body and mind

Goal Setting Made Easy (www.relfe.com/goal_setting.html)

Writing what you want creates a kind of miracle. This probably works in the following manner. When you first think of something, it is just a thought in your head. It is not yet in the physical universe. However, thought is energy and the universe and everything in it are also made of energy. When you write something down, your thought now exists in the physical universe. Somehow, the physical universe eventually follows suit. Many intuitive people know that thought creates reality. If you need scientific, rational reasoning as to why this works, I suggest you read "The Holographic Universe" by Michael Talbot.

Herbal Healer (www.herbalhealer.com)

Herbal Healer Academy Inc., is a private membership organization, offering alternative natural medicine, herbs, homeopathics, tinctures, health books, videos, flower essences, essential oils, soap kits, hair analysis, private correspondence consultations, ear coning, herbal teas, soaps, shampoos, natural pet products, and more to make your life safer and healthier.

Dr. Joseph Mercola (www.mercola.com)

"How to Achieve High Level Health and Wellness without Expensive Drugs or Surgery." Your body is designed to self regulate and be healthy. If this sounds like a preposterous statement, then you have been a victim of a disease-focused mass media controlled by powerful special interests that wants to convince you that expensive drugs and surgery are the logical choices when confronting health challenges.

When you shine a bright light in a dark corner you remove the darkness. You simply can't have light and darkness simultaneously. Similarly when you focus on health, disease dramatically disappears. Disease and health can't co-exist.

When you focus on choosing natural unprocessed foods, healthy water, air, appropriate sun exposure, exercise, proper rest, emotional balancing and avoidance of toxic chemicals and pollutants, you will shine the light on disease and allow health to replace it.

Dr. Hulda Clark (www.drclark.com)

Parasite Cleanse, Kidney Cleanse, Intestinal Cleanse, Liver Flush
Dr. Clark's four cleanses are an important part of her protocol. Dr. Clark recommends them for healthy persons too, on a regular basis, to keep the body in shape.

Kripalu Yoga (www.kripalu.org)

Kripalu Center is an institution where people can come to discover what it means to be fully human and fully alive through a nonsectarian and nondogmatic approach to yoga. We are dedicated to the honest and unfettered inquiry into, and pursuit of, all philosophies, techniques, and approaches that produce thriving in the individual, the family, the institution, the business, the community, the society, and the planet—all at the same time.

News and Activism

Our Stolen Future (www.ourstolenfuture.org)

The book *Our Stolen Future* brought world-wide attention to scientific discoveries about endocrine disruption and the fact that common contaminants can interfere with the natural signals controlling development of the fetus. This website tracks the most recent developments.

Defenders of Wildlife (www.defenders.org)

Defenders of Wildlife is dedicated to the protection of all native wild animals and plants in their natural communities. We focus our programs on what scientists consider two of the most serious environmental threats to the planet: the accelerating rate of extinction of species and the associated loss of biological diversity, and habitat alteration and destruction. Long known for our leadership on endangered species issues, Defenders of Wildlife also advocates new approaches to wildlife conservation that will help keep species from becoming endangered. Our programs encourage protection of entire ecosystems and interconnected habitats while protecting predators that serve as indicator species for ecosystem health.

The Humane Society University (http://tinyurl.com/hsuniv)

Humane Society University offers B.S. degrees and graduate certificates in Animal Studies, Animal Policy and Advocacy, and Humane Leadership. Humane Society University is committed to providing academically rigorous, interdisciplinary, distance learning degree programs related to animals that promote personal, intellectual, and professional growth. The university has recruited leading scholars in the field to its faculty. HSU seeks to attract students who wish to be on the forefront of creating a more humane society and to give them the tools they need to succeed.

The Wilderness Society (www.wilderness.org)

We're spirited people protecting America's Wilderness since 1935 through the potent combination of science, advocacy and education.

Other works

A Woman's Guide to Bikes and Biking (1999)

This book in your hands is *that* book brought to life.

Tripping with Gabrielle (2010)

Tripping With Gabrielle is a story of one woman's soul survival. Gabrielle is a German adoptee who begins life early on with a biological father who is so abusive he tries to kill her the night she is born. She is placed into a Catholic orphanage that provides a minimal amount of childcare, including one diaper change per day. Fortune shines upon this little baby when her real father and mother, a special Army couple, find and immediately fall in love with her. Gabrielle finally leaves Germany on a ship with her new family, and begins her American journey into the angst ridden, child then teenage world that we know as the USA.

Gabrielle is every mother's nightmare, as she loves to call herself. She screams so much that at age 12 she permanently damages her vocal chords. She hates herself so much she creates bruises on her face by punching herself. She fights with local boys, and sniffs paint with local girls. Gabrielle's runaway stories begin at age seven and finally end after several years on the road, as a hitchhiker. But all is not lost in Gabrielle's life. She finds her soul amidst the garbage of her mind, and eventually, through the Grace of God and her mother's prayers, she discovers inner healing. Believe it or not, this is a funny story. Gabrielle's many antics will have you holding your sides laughing out loud. Her sad moments will leave you crying crocodile tears. Her moments of joy will make you rejoice with her. There's a magical world out there, filled with wonderful people and not so wonderful spirits.

Join Gabrielle as she meets a cast of characters that range geographically from Lawless, Oklahoma to Berlin, Germany. Trip out with the redwood trees in Mendocino County, California where Gabrielle makes her home in a tree stump house. Feel the feathery softness of five foot high ferns in her majestic forest home deep in the woods of Albion, California. Bathe with Gabrielle in the river as it meets the ocean. Feel her joy, her sadness, her awakening, her truth as she experiences all that life has to offer, yet owns no possessions, nor does she have a home. Gabrielle's feet will walk many miles before she overcomes addictions such as eating disorders, alcohol and drugs. Her spirit is led by a white pony named Snowflake, and by the many wonderful beings she meets who help her on her journey. Dog friends accompany her during her travels, in fact, they save her and protect her from what lurks beyond in the scary, dark sadness of her soul.

Gabrielle finally finds success in life by helping other homeless abandoned abused children, and realizes that her true place can be found in the heart of the universe, in the Light of the Father and in the love of His son. Gabrielle's belief system isn't exclusive, she welcomes witches, Buddhists, Moonies, Hare Krishnas and Spiritualists. She realizes that all people's beliefs and stories are equally true. Most importantly, love is the answer, the final glue that holds us all together. By experiencing enough love, Gabrielle finally is healed and can come home. Tripping with Gabrielle is a wild ride you won't want to miss. We'll call it a fiction but you can always imagine that there must be some truth to her story. Names, dates, places are all changed to protect the guilty. Gabrielle assumes responsibility for her follies, and hopes her story will help others find their way out of the muck, the gore, the filth that sometimes blocks our soul's progress into the Light of Love that is our birthright.

Jules has personally experienced traveling down the homeless hitchhiker road. She is grateful to have lived in the same home for the past 16 years, her longest time in one place. *Tripping With Gabrielle* is Jules' manifesto to the homeless, runaways, the disenchanted, the addicted, the helpless and the poor of the world. She salutes you.